FLEETBOOK NO. 1

Buses of GREATER MANCHESTER
6th edition 1983

Edited and published by
A M WITTON
Room 20 City Buildings
69 Corporation Street
Manchester M4 2DE

6th edition revised and enlarged 1983 - ISBN 0 86047 016 4
(1st edition 'Greater Manchester Transport Buses and Coaches' 1974 - ISBN 0 86047 000 8)
(2nd edition revised and enlarged 1975 - ISBN 0 86047 001 6)
(3rd edition revised and enlarged 1977 - ISBN 0 86047 013 X)
(4th edition revised 1978 - ISBN 0 86047 014 8)
(5th edition revised 1980 - ISBN 0 86047 015 6)
Copyright 1983 by A M Witton

Introduction

We are seeing in Greater Manchester the last stages of that process which took place in London in the 1930s - with a large public authority, having inherited an enormously varied fleet from numerous acquired undertakings, steadily concentrating its purchases on a handful of standard types. In London that resulted in types which, though numerous then, would nowadays be considered worthy candidates for inclusion in rally programmes or museum guides. In Manchester, the ubiquitous 'Standards' - now over 1,700 of them including the identical buses acquired from Lancashire United - have not reached the age where they receive the veneration due to antiquity. None has been withdrawn, though one has lost its roof to replace the truly venerable open-topper 5995. They demonstrate that to be efficient and well-managed, a large undertaking must often take decisions which will hardly endear it to enthusiasts, most of whom favour variety and traditional design in vehicles. That thousands of copies of each edition of this book find a ready market, testifies that despite increasing standardisation, Greater Manchester is still a happy hunting ground for enthusiasts, some of whom are doubtless too young to remember the patchwork of undertakings and colour schemes that existed before 1969.

The last few of those thousands of buses which came from the municipal fleets in 1969, are still in the PTE's stock, but they will not last much longer. Similarly the individualistic lines of the former North Western fleet will soon be no more than a memory, jogged from time to time by visits to the Boyle Street museum. Only the 25 Bristol VRs ordered by North Western and delivered to SELNEC remain unscathed - and they may well be on the scrap-line by the time our next edition comes out.

The Lancashire United takeover in 1981 did at least cause a brief growth in variety in the PTE fleet, with Seddons, Leyland Leopard buses and ex-London DMSs joining their 'standard' cousins. But LUT had practised the PTE's standardisation policy for several years, and most of the ex-LUT buses likely to last any length of time with the PTE are - you've guessed it - Northern Counties-bodied 'Fleetlines' and Leyland Nationals. A handful of Guy 'Arabs', once the mainstay of LUT, just scraped into PTE ownership en route to an early appointment with the scrap-heap.

Standardisation is only a relative concept, and Greater Manchester's 'standard' buses do not meet the criteria as well as, say, the RT or RM classes of London Transport. They are based on two chassis makes paired with two makes of bodies, of which all four possible permutations are in service. There are numerous detail differences which the sharp-eyed will notice, in such matters as number and layout of opening windows, design of windscreens, and interior trim. Since 1981, Greater Manchester's first completely new bus livery since the foundation of SELNEC in 1969 has gained wide acceptance and, mingling in the streets with buses bearing the older orange and off-white livery, have given us at least a shadow of the pre-1969 splash of colour. And, of course, Greater Manchester is an inveterate buyer of experimental and non-standard buses. Four Dennis 'Dominators', a Leyland 'Olympian', three Ailsa-Volvos and fifteen Leyland 'Titans' give the fleet variety if you know where to look for them; while the 170 MCW 'Metrobuses', with 20 more on order, have become almost a 'standard' class of their own. The most spectacular news is that two Kassbohrer/Setra coaches are on order for the Central Coaching Unit! Standardisation, indeed!

The other undertakings in Greater Manchester still merit interest by enthusiasts with National Travel (West) acquiring a pair of Dennis 'Falcons' - the first

Dennis single-deckers to be acquired by any of National Travel (West)'s numerous forebears since 1938, when North Western took delivery of a pair of Dennis 'Lancet' buses! Yelloway continues to stick loyally to Plaxton coachwork, while accommodating itself to the need to replace its AECs gradually by Leylands. Mayne's has developed, with PTE recognition, a second regular stage service into the heart of Manchester since our last edition came out; it has also learnt from its associate company, Cooper's of Warrington, about the possibilities of rebuilding elderly underfloor-engined chassis to produce modern luxury coaches. No chance of boredom in that direction! Indeed, to resume the London analogy with which we started, Mayne's survival as a stage operator in the heart of one of Britain's largest cities is as if Partridge's Chocolate Express, or Dangerfield's Overground, had escaped the London Transport takeover net and operated busy urban routes into the 1980s! Of course, the legislative framework in London has been very different from that in Manchester. But those Southern enthusiasts who mourn the passing of the 1920s in London could do worse than spend a few hours with a camera in Manchester's Stevenson Square.

The two newcomers to this book operate express services only incidentally to their main calling as tour operators. Shearings, now having given up their share of the British Coachways consortium, operate a daily but not frequent service between Manchester Airport and Liverpool. The Blundell group, personified by their Webster subsidiary, run a number of seasonal express services from the Wigan area. Between them they demonstrate that, although to construct a financially viable express service overnight is almost impossible, the long-established holiday routes can still pay respectable dividends. On the vehicle front, Shearing's long-term dependence on Fords has been reduced by the recent arrival of DAFs and Leyland 'Leopards'; while Smith's, with a more innovative approach to vehicle development in past years, still rebuild the occasional AEC 'Reliance' chassis to keep the tradition alive.

We have said it before, but it needs saying every time; don't put yourself or other road users in danger as you pursue your hobby; and don't ever trespass on private land. One company featured in this book has asked us to make plain that enthusiast visitors to their garage are admitted only by prior appointment. This does not mean that you can walk in anywhere else! All bus and coach operators appreciate the courtesy of a letter or phone-call in advance to arrange a visit; some, including the PTE, will admit only organised parties, which is fair enough when you realise that the PTE has to turn out well over 2,000 buses for service every rush hour, and unplanned visits to garages would interfere with the primary task of moving passengers. We hear a few stories that indicate that some busmen consider enthusiasts a 'pain in the neck', or perhaps in some other part of the anatomy. Don't ever do anything that could lend currency to this view. Keep to pavements in bus stations and streets; no bus driver can be expected to reckon with a camera-wielding lunatic jumping out from blind corners! Play safe - survive - have fun; but not at someone else's expense.

Finally, our thanks are due to the staff of all the undertakings featured in this book. Many of these people are enthusiasts themselves; all have shown forbearance and patience in coping with often near-impossible requests for information! The publications of the PSV Circle have been extensively consulted in compiling this book; we recommend to the serious enthusiast that membership of the PSV Circle or the Omnibus Society is money well spent. We try to ensure that every 'Fleetbook' is as accurate as possible; if you are one of those who takes delight in spotting mistakes, please let us know of any you find, but please also tell us the source of your information.

We use the standard codes for bodywork variations as follows:-

Preceding the seating capacity figure		Following the seating capacity figure	
B	- Single-deck bus	D	- Front entrance and centre exit
C	- Single-deck coach	F	- Front entrance/exit
CH	- Double-deck highbridge coach	FT	- Front entrance/exit and fitted
DP	- Single-deck dual-purpose vehicle		with toilet (usually at rear)
H	- Double-deck highbridge bus		
O	- Double-deck open-top bus		

A M Witton
Manchester, December 1982

Greater Manchester Transport

Although the Greater Manchester PTE was formed only in April 1974 from the former SELNEC and Wigan Corporation undertakings, its history can be said to have commenced 150 years earlier. In 1824 a toll-collector named John Greenwood, attracted by the amount of carriage traffic passing through his toll gate, started a horse omnibus service between Manchester and Pendleton, charging the relatively expensive fare of 6d; like most early horse-bus proprietors Greenwood carried mainly well-to-do patrons. It was a success, and soon there were groups of horse-bus services in many parts of Manchester. Many of these were eventually merged into the Manchester Tramways and Carriage Co Ltd, in which Greenwood himself was a leading light.

In 1877 the Company began horse tram operations in the Salford area, and these were rapidly extended. Its powers to build and operate tramways were granted under the Tramways Act 1870, under which each local council through whose area the line passed had the right to compulsorily purchase the tramways after 21 years, and every seventh year thereafter. At about the turn of the century, with most of these 21-year periods coming to an end, the tramways of Greater Manchester fell into municipal ownership in a very short period, between 1899 and 1904; the heart of the network, in the cities of Manchester and Salford, was purchased by the two city councils in 1901. Not all the tramways were served by horse cars; steam trams were run by the Bury, Rochdale & Oldham Tramway Co from 1883 between those three towns, and the Wigan & District Tramways Co had introduced steam trams to Wigan in 1882. However, within a few years of municipalisation, virtually all tramway mileage in the area had been electrified.

One completely new tram network, owned by the Stalybridge, Hyde, Mossley and Dukinfield (SHMD) Joint Board, was set up in 1904 by agreement between these four towns, and started to run electric trams later the same year. New tramway construction was also undertaken at about this time by the South Lancashire company, which eventually became part of Lancashire United Transport; its vast system, mostly single-track, eventually stretched from the edge of Manchester to Prescot near Liverpool. Of Greater Manchester's municipal transport undertakings only two, Leigh and Ramsbottom, never ran their own trams. Leigh obtained tramway construction powers in 1903 but never used them, relying instead on the South Lancashire company's trams (between 1902 and 1933) and later the SLT trolleybuses; Leigh Corporation developed a small motorbus network for routes not served by SLT. Ramsbottom ran a small trolleybus installation between 1913 and 1931.

The new municipal undertakings were quick to establish through services across each other's frontiers, and these are still reflected in today's bus routes. As all the principal tramways were of standard gauge with overhead electrification (there was some narrow-gauge trackage in Wigan), and as nearly all had through trackage linking with neighbouring towns, through running over long distances was feasible. As late as 1930 a Liverpool tram visited Ashton-under-Lyne, a distance of some 45 miles, for a special event! The regular through workings were shorter, but still impressive.

Trolleybuses came early to Greater Manchester, but the first few trolleybus experiments lacked staying power. They included the Stockport to Offerton route of 1913-1919, which used the Lloyd-Kohler system with detachable trolleys running on a single pair of roadside wires; the vehicles had to stop, detach and exchange their trolleys whenever they met. More orthodox but even more short-lived was the Oldham - Ashton joint service which ran through for only one year (August 1925 - September 1926), although the section within Ashton continued until 1938. As mentioned above, Ramsbottom ran a Holcombe Brook - Edenfield trolleybus service until 1931. Wigan replaced a narrow-gauge tramway, to Markland Mill, with the town's only trolleybus service, which ran between 1925 and 1931.

Two more successful trolleybus installations were the extensive South Lancashire Transport system, which replaced that company's trams on a number of routes, and the network of services established by Manchester and Ashton Corporations from 1938 onwards.

The SLT trolleybus system was designed to replace the far-flung tram network operated by the company and referred to above. The tramways needed renewal, and in many cases doubling of the track would have been desirable but was not possible because of the narrowness of the roads. So the decision was reached to replace most of the SLT tram services with trolleybuses. An Act of Parliament granted the necessary powers, and also authorised a change of name from 'South Lancashire Tramways' to 'South Lancashire Transport'; the company's parent, Lancashire United Tramways Ltd, had similarly been renamed 'Lancashire United Transport' in 1928. The inaugural trolleybus run from Atherton to Ashton-in-Makerfield took place on 28th July 1930, and conversion of most of the tram routes to trolleybuses followed rapidly. However, the Farnworth - Pendlebury and Leigh - Lowton sections were replaced by motorbuses, and various lines in the Farnworth and Worsley areas were handed over for municipal operation while remaining SLT property. 1931 saw trolleybuses introduced on a new linked service from Atherton to Farnworth via Swinton; at 14¼ miles this service, though far from direct, was the third longest trolleybus route ever operated in Britain. The last SLT tram ran on the Leigh - Bolton service on 16th December 1933. Bolton Corporation ran their own trams on the Bolton section of this route until 1936. In that year they were replaced by four trolleybuses, physically identical to the rest of the SLT fleet and garaged at Atherton, but bought and operated on behalf of Bolton Corporation - the only trolleybuses ever owned by that town.

The Manchester/Ashton trolleybus system linked the city centre with Ashton, Stalybridge and Hyde (Gee Cross) in the east; New Moston in the north-east; and a circuitous route from the city centre via the inner eastern suburbs of Ancoats and Ardwick to Greenheys in the south. There was also a route from Ashton, crossing the Hyde route at Denton and continuing to Haughton Green. Most of the services have been extended or modified to take advantage of the greater operating flexibility of the motorbus, but the shape of the trolleybus system can still be discerned in present bus routes 123, 210, 216, 218, 219, 347 and 348; the New Moston routes were covered by extending various existing motorbus services. By 1960 several of the trolleybus routes had been replaced by motorbuses, and the last trolleybuses in Greater Manchester ran in 1966; the SLT trolleybuses had finished long before, in 1958.

The tram remained the backbone of Greater Manchester's municipal transport for about three decades. The first blow to its supremacy came in 1930, when Manchester's busy route 53, restricted to single-deck tramcars by a low bridge, was converted to motorbuses. A longer-term threat to the trams had appeared from 1928, when the municipal and company operators began a system of limited-stop motorbuses, offering fast transport along the main tram routes and penetrating further into newer suburbs and sometimes open country. These services were linked across the centre of Manchester at first, until these links were broken at the request of the Traffic Commissioners. The private bus companies such as North Western and LUT took a large part in this operation. One firm which nowadays specialises in coaching - Yelloway of Rochdale - pioneered the Rochdale - Royton - Manchester limited-stop bus service, which was transferred to a consortium of Manchester, Oldham and Rochdale Corporations in 1944, together with several vehicles; it is still operated as PTE services 23/24. Several other independent companies, mostly quite small, competed with the municipal bus services in the 1920s and 1930s; the last of these to disappear was John Sharp of Longsight, whose Manchester - Woodford service (the basis of present service 190) was taken over by Manchester and Stockport Corporations in 1936.

The first Greater Manchester towns to abandon trams completely were Wigan in 1931, Rochdale in 1932 and Ashton-under-Lyne in 1938. Elsewhere, tramway abandonment was already under way in 1939 but was then halted by the wartime shortage of motor fuel. The process was restarted after the war. The SHMD Board ran its last tram in 1945, although it still provided trackage for Manchester and Stockport trams until 1947; its commitment to maintaining electrical overhead remained as it supplied current for trolleybuses on the Stalybridge and Hyde routes until they were abandoned in the 1960s. However, SHMD never ran trolleybuses of its own. Oldham abandoned trams in 1946, Bolton and Salford in 1947 and Bury in 1949. The last Manchester tram route (number 35 between Exchange and Hazel Grove, the forerunner of the present 192 bus route) was closed in January 1949, with appropriate fanfare. There remained only the Stockport trams, which continued to run between Levenshulme and Hazel Grove until 1950, and to Vernon Park, Edgeley, Cheadle Heath and Reddish until 1951, when they too passed into history.

Large numbers of motorbuses were needed to make good wartime losses and replace the last trams; this resulted, especially in Manchester and Salford, in the creation of distinctive bus designs for each town. Manchester bought large fleets of Leylands, Daimlers and locally-built Crossleys, all fitted with bodies similar to the Crossley design of the period, though several other manufacturers built them as well. Stockport, Crossley's home town, bought Crossleys and Leylands with bodywork by the manufacturers to the latter's standard designs. Rochdale plumped mainly for AECs; the SHMD Board, which before the war had opted for the unusual Thornycroft make, switched to Daimlers and Atkinsons. Leigh had AECs and Leylands all with low-height bodies; later this undertaking tried Dennis 'Lolines' and AEC 'Renowns'. Bury went mainly for Leylands apart from the solitary Guy 'Wulfrunian', the only one to work for a Greater Manchester municipality, though one other was owned by LUT. Salford at one time had a fleet made up almost entirely of Daimlers fitted with Metro-Cammell bodies with straight staircases, of a distinctly classical appearance. The other fleets went mainly for Leylands, often with a contribution from Crossley in the early post-war period.

Among the larger companies which still ran important services in Greater Manchester, the North Western Road Car Co ran a fleet of Bristols and Leylands, the former including some rebodied pre-war specimens. LUT stuck to Guys, of which the latest Guy 'Arab' Mk Vs survived into PTE ownership in 1981, and were withdrawn only recently. The various colour schemes of the municipal and company operators, all but two of whom ran into the centre of the conurbation, made places like Piccadilly and Greengate an attractive riot of colour, which the pleasant but stereotyped PTE livery has failed to perpetuate!

After one-man operation of double-deckers became legal in 1965, the trickle of rear-engined double-deckers into the area's fleets soon became a flood. Manchester Corporation led the way in 1966 by converting several suburban routes to one-man double-deck operation; within a year this type of vehicle had started to replace crew-operated buses on busy routes into the heart of Manchester. One-man operation is now predominant in Greater Manchester, although there are still significant numbers of crew-operated services.

From the 1930s onwards, various attempts had been made to co-ordinate the Greater Manchester undertakings into a single Board, like the London Passenger Transport Board which had been established in 1933. However, as few services were operated by independent undertakings, and as the municipal and company operators had been markedly successful in linking their services and offering through fares, the matter was not as urgent as in London; perhaps it was for this reason that so little progress was made. The Transport Act 1968 provided for transfer of municipal bus fleets in the four largest English conurbations, excluding London, to Passenger Transport Executives. The result in Greater Manchester was the SELNEC (South-East Lancashire and North-East Cheshire) Passenger Transport Executive, which was set up in October 1969; one month later it took over some 2,500 buses of nine different makes from the 11 vesting undertakings (Ashton-under-Lyne, Bolton, Bury, Leigh, Manchester, Oldham, Ramsbottom, Rochdale, Salford and Stockport transport departments and the SHMD Board). Of these, the largest was Manchester itself, and the smallest was the 12-bus fleet of Ramsbottom UDC. A unique contribution to the fleet was SHMD's no. 70, the only double-deck Atkinson ever built, which has since been preserved. Daimler and Leyland between them provided the lion's share of the vehicles.

Fleet standardisation was obviously an urgent need. Within a couple of years the first prototypes arrived of the 'SELNEC standard' double-deck bus, based on Leyland 'Atlantean' and Daimler 'Fleetline' chassis with bodywork by Northern Counties and Park Royal. When present orders are complete there will be some 1,900 of these in service accounting for nearly all the undertaking's double-deck requirements. Among experimental vehicles bought in small numbers were 10 Scania 'Metropolitans', 2 Mercedes/Northern Counties integral single-deckers and 2 Foden/Northern Counties semi-integral double-deckers; these have now been withdrawn. The standard single-decker was chosen by trials of 12 Scania and 12 Leyland National single-deckers on an assortment of routes in all parts of Greater Manchester. The Leyland National won the day and some 180 of these, including the original batch and those acquired from LUT in 1981, are now in service. The Scanias were concentrated on Leigh garage with certain other non-standard single-deckers, and withdrawals of these have now started.

Special vehicle requirements were catered for by a batch of Seddon 'midibuses' for Manchester's 'Centreline' and other services in cramped areas. Two different battery-electric buses, one 'midi' and one full-sized single-decker, have been tried and have given demonstration runs for other undertakings as far afield as the United States, but have now been sold. Recent small-scale purchases have included several Dennis 'Dominators' and Ailsa-Volvo AB55s, together with a prototype Leyland 'Olympian', forerunner of a planned initial batch of 25. Fifteen Leyland 'Titans' were bought before production ceased at the Park Royal factory, and 170 MCW 'Metrobuses' are now in stock, and are used widely in the central, southern and eastern parts of the operating area.

Until March 1972, many services in the south and east of Greater Manchester were provided by the North Western Road Car Co Ltd. 'North Western' was descended from the Macclesfield area operations of the British Automobile Traction Co, which were started in 1913 and passed to the BAT's Peak District Committee in 1922 and to the newly-formed North Western company in 1923. The head office was moved from Macclesfield to Stockport later in 1923, and remained in Stockport throughout North Western's separate existence. It grew rapidly and developed many stage and express services in the Cheshire and Derbyshire areas, the dormitory towns of Altrincham, Urmston, Flixton and Partington, and the hilly country east of Oldham and the Tameside towns. Many of its services were jointly operated with the Greater Manchester municipal undertakings; on one of them, the Manchester - Ashton - Glossop route, North Western had no fewer than three municipal partners! With the establishment of SELNEC the situation was ripe for tidying up. SELNEC purchased that part of the North Western business which ran stage routes in the PTE area, involving garages at Altrincham, Glossop, Oldham, Stockport and Urmston, in 1972. The rural routes in Derbyshire, based at Buxton and Matlock, were transferred to Trent, while those in Cheshire operated from Macclesfield, Northwich and Warrington went to Crosville. The remainder - the express coach business - was kept by the NBC and used to form the nucleus of today's National Travel (West) Ltd company, whose fleet and history is featured elsewhere in this book.

Local government reorganisation brought SELNEC under the control of the new Greater Manchester Metropolitan County in April 1974. At first the only visible signs of the new change were the replacement of the SELNEC fleetnames with the 'wavy M' logo and 'Greater Manchester Transport' inscription, and the adoption of a slightly darker shade of orange for the orange and off-white livery inherited from SELNEC. Livery experiments were made with a variety of different applications of orange and white; many LUT buses received a 'more orange' livery after LUT had been acquired as a subsidiary by the PTE. The Titans and the first batches of Metrobuses arrived in their own versions of the 'more orange' livery. These experiments culminated in the recent introduction of a colour scheme of orange, dark brown and white which is now progressively being applied to all vehicles.

The Greater Manchester County has slightly different boundaries from those of the SELNEC designated area. In particular, Wigan was added to the new authority, and Wigan's fleet of maroon and white liveried buses were transferred to PTE control on 1st April 1974, becoming a local district of Greater Manchester Transport. However, the PTE still operates local buses in several areas, such as Glossop, Wilmslow and Poynton, which are outside the new county; it also participates in jointly-run services to places well outside, such as Warrington, Chorley, Rawtenstall and even Liverpool. The LUT takeover has of course greatly increased the area within which Greater Manchester buses are commonplace; LUT has long been the major operator in areas like Earlestown and Newton-le-Willows in the County of Merseyside.

SELNEC had acquired fourteen Bedford coaches from Manchester City Transport in 1969, and these were used as the nucleus of what is now an extensive coaching operation. They were joined by the only other full coaching-standard vehicle acquired by SELNEC at formation – Salford's Transport Committee coach, an AEC 'Reliance' with Weymann Fanfare bodywork, which had attained its seventh year in 1969 with amazingly little mileage on the clock! The initial commitments were the Manchester Airport express coach link to central Manchester; SELNEC soon added an 'executive express' coach service for City commuters from Halebarns, and a much more ambitious scheme, the 'Trans-Lancs Express' service linking the ring of towns surrounding Manchester. This 32-mile service is still worked, generally on an hourly frequency, though its increasing popularity has outstripped the seat availability of coaches and so ordinary double-deckers are now used.

The coaches were also made available to build up a private-hire, holidays and tours market. Originally called 'SELNEC Travel', the name was changed under Greater Manchester Transport to 'Charterplan'. The Charterplan business is part of the PTE's undertaking but has its own management, fleet and premises situated at the former North Western company's head office at Charles Street, Stockport. The Bury-based coaching business of Warburton's was taken over on 1st November 1975, and several vehicles of the Central Coaching Unit (Charterplan) carry Warburton's fleetnames and livery and are based at Bury garage.

Greater Manchester Transport acquired control of Lancashire United Transport Ltd with effect from 1st January 1976, and of Godfrey Abbott Group Ltd (together with the joint PTE/Godfrey Abbott offshoot, Dial-a-Ride Ltd) with effect from November 1976.

LUT started life as the financial holding company which controlled the South Lancashire Tramways system. In 1906 it opened its first motorbus services, in the Leigh area, but these were not a success and operated for only a short while before withdrawal. Motorbus operation was resumed in 1919 and the fleet grew rapidly to 152 buses, including some double-deckers, by 1929. The replacement of the SLT trams by trolleybuses has already been mentioned, but a wide-ranging motorbus system was built up, mainly in the areas covered by the present metropolitan boroughs of Salford, Bolton and Wigan, with extensive operations to the west of Greater Manchester as well. For a short while after trolleybuses were abandoned in 1958, the replacing motorbuses ran with LUT fleetnames but SLT legal lettering. The standard LUT bus was the Guy, but Atkinsons, Daimlers and Seddons among others formed part of the post-war fleet. After the PTE took control, new vehicles purchases came to consist of 'standard' type Fleetlines for double-deck work, Leyland National single-deck buses and Leyland Leopard coaches; however, LUT's 'swan song', the last new vehicles to be purchased by LUT as a separate undertaking, were three Volvo coaches which arrived in 1980. LUT was completely merged into the main PTE undertaking with effect from 1st April 1981.

The history of the Godfrey Abbott Group goes back to 1948, when Mr W Godfrey Abbott founded a one-vehicle, one-man concern. Several local coach firms in Sale and Altrincham were taken over, including Altrincham Coachways Ltd, formerly a subsidiary of the North Western company, in 1966. The Godfrey Abbott firm was instrumental, together with Greater Manchester PTE, in setting up Dial-a-Ride Ltd, which started trading in 1974 to provide a demand-actuated minibus service between the various districts of Sale, with a fleet of minibuses mostly of the Bedford CF type. The service was operated from Godfrey Abbott's headquarters in Cross Street, Sale, where a radio control point was established for the minibus fleet. Intending passengers could phone the control room giving their desired boarding and destination points, and a suitable bus would be called by radio to collect them.

Another pioneering activity by Abbott's was a service from Manchester to Paris, started on 22nd May 1976; it has since been transferred to joint operation by Greater Manchester PTE, Grey-Green Coaches and Les Cars Express of Amiens, France. In 1979 the Godfrey Abbott coach fleet was moved from Sale to the Charterplan headquarters at Charles Street, Stockport, and acquired PTE fleet numbers while retaining their Godfrey Abbott fleetnames and livery. In 1981 the Dial-a-Ride service, whose vehicles and staff had been left in sole possession of the Sale depot, was closed down, and six of the ten vehicles then owned were transferred to PTE stock but have since been withdrawn.

All Central Coaching Unit vehicles are painted in eye-catching liveries of white with different coloured flashes to denote the fleet - brown and orange (Charterplan), lime green and olive green (Godfrey Abbott), two shades of blue (Warburton's) or red and yellow (Lancashire United). These liveries are distinguished in the lists which follow by the suffixes 'c', 'g', 'w' or 'l' to the fleet numbers of the appropriate coaches. In addition, several coaches of the main PTE fleet now run in a blue, white and orange livery for Manchester Airport service 200, and these are shown in the lists suffixed 'a'. Coaches shown without suffixes remain allocated to the main PTE fleet and carry standard orange or orange/brown liveries as applied to buses. 'Airport' coaches are allocated to Northenden garage and belong to the main fleet, not the Coaching Unit. These suffixes are unofficial and are not shown on the vehicles.

Most main fleet vehicles carry two-letter garage codes at front and rear adjacent to the fleet number; Coaching Unit vehicles may be presumed to be allocated to Bury (Warburton's), Atherton (Lancashire United) or Charles Street, Stockport. A list of the garage codes and the garages to which they refer is given below. The principal garage in each group is given first, followed by the names of any subsidiary garages which use the same code.

AM - ALTRINCHAM Oakfield Street	NN - NORTHENDEN Harling Road
AN - ATHERTON Howe Bridge	OM - OLDHAM Wallshaw Street
BN - BOLTON Crook Street	PS - MANCHESTER Princess Road
BS - MANCHESTER Birchfields Road	RE - ROCHDALE Mellor Street
BY - BURY Rochdale Road	SN - SWINTON Partington Lane
FK - SALFORD Frederick Road	ST - STOCKPORT Daw Bank
HE - MANCHESTER Hyde Road	STOCKPORT Charles Street (coaches)
HY - HINDLEY Capps Street, Platt Bridge	TE - ASHTON-UNDER-LYNE Whitelands Road
LH - LEIGH Holden Road	GLOSSOP York Street

WE – WEASTE Eccles New Road   WN – WIGAN Melverley Street

The head office for the entire undertaking is situated at 2 Devonshire Street North, Ardwick, adjacent to HE garage. On the same plot of land stands the Central Works, where Manchester trams and buses have been overhauled (and sometimes whole bodies have been built!) since the Manchester Corporation undertaking started in 1901. Facilities for running maintenance also exist at all garage premises, and major overhauls can be carried out at BN and ST in addition to the Central Works.

1-2

Chassis: Leyland 'Leopard' PSU5C/4R built 1978
Body: (1) Duple C55F (2) Duple C48F

| 1c | ANA 1T | 2c | ANA 2T |

3-4

Chassis: Leyland 'Leopard' PSU3E/4R built 1978
Body: (3) Duple C44F (4) Duple C51F

| 3c | ANA 3T | 4w | ANA 4T |

5-19

Chassis: AEC 'Reliance' 6U3ZR built 1976-1978
Body: (5-9) Plaxton C53F
        (16) Plaxton C40FT
        (17/18) Plaxton C44FT
        (19) Duple C41FT

5g	ANA 5T	8g	ANA 8T	16g	RVU 536R	18g	RVU 539R
6g	ANA 6T	9g	ANA 9T	17g	RVU 537R	19g	MJA 900P
7g	ANA 7T						

21-24

Chassis: Leyland 'Tiger' TRCTL11/3R built 1982 and on order
Body: Duple C46FT

| 21c | BJA 856Y | 22c | | 23c | | 24c | |

26-27

Chassis: Leyland 'Leopard' PSU5D/4R built 1980
Body: (26) Duple C32FT (27) Duple C42F

| 26g | MNC 500W | 27w | MNC 501W |

28-29

Chassis: Leyland 'Leopard' PSU3F/4R built 1980
Body: Duple C44F

| 28c | MNC 502W | 29c | MNC 503W |

30-31

Chassis and Body: Kassbohrer/Setra S215HD integral-construction coaches with C49FT bodies, on order for 1983 delivery

| 30c | | 31c | |

35-48

Chassis: Leyland 'Leopard' PSU3E/4R built 1977-1979
Body: Plaxton C51F
Ex Lancashire United Transport Nos. 480-484/537-541/566-569 in 1981

35a	OTD 824R	39w	OTD 828R	431	TWH 688T	461	YBN 630V
~~36a~~	~~OTD 825R~~	401	TWH 685T	441	TWH 689T	471	YBN 631V
~~37a~~	~~OTD 826R~~	411	TWH 686T	451	YBN 629V	481	YBN 632V
~~38a~~	~~OTD 827R~~	421	TWH 687T				

49-51

Chassis: Volvo B58/61 built 1980
Body: Plaxton C55F
Ex Lancashire United Transport Nos. 614-616 in 1981

49l	DEN 245W	50c	DEN 246W	51c	DEN 247W

56-81

Chassis: Leyland 'Leopard' PSU3B/4R built 1973-1975
Body: (56-04) ECW C47F
(70-75) Plaxton C49F
(76-78) Duple C51F
(79) Duple C44F
(80/81) ECW C49F

56	AJA 357L	62	AWH 62L	72	XNE 884L	78c	YNA 399M
57	AJA 358L	63	AWH 63L	73	XNE 887L	79w	YNA 400M
58	AJA 359L	64	AWH 64L	76c	YNA 397M	80	HNE 640N
60	AJA 361L	70a	XNE 882L	77	YNA 398M	81	HNE 641N
61	AJA 362L	71a	XNE 883L				

82-88

Chassis: Leyland 'Leopard' PSU3B/4R, rebuilt from earlier chassis in 1981/1982
Body: Duple C51F built 1981/1982

82c	SND 82X	84w	SND 84X	86c	SND 86X	88g	SND 88X
83c	SND 83X	85w	SND 85X	87g	SND 87X		

101-170

Chassis and Body: Leyland National 10351/1R integral-construction vehicles with B41F bodies, built 1975

101	HNB 20N	119	HNE 649N	136	JNA 592N	153	KBU 890P
102	HNB 21N	120	HNE 650N	137	JNA 593N	154	KBU 891P
103	HNB 22N	121	HNE 651N	138	JNA 594N	155	KBU 892P
104	HNB 23N	122	HNE 652N	139	JNA 595N	156	JVM 980N
105	HNB 24N	123	HJA 127N	140	JNA 596N	157	JVM 981N
106	HNB 46N	124	HJA 128N	141	JNA 597N	158	KBU 893P
107	HNB 47N	125	HJA 129N	142	JNA 598N	159	KBU 894P
108	HNB 45N	126	HJA 130N	143	JNA 599N	160	KBU 895P
109	HNE 633N	127	HJA 131N	144	JNA 600N	161	KBU 896P
110	HNE 634N	128	JNA 584N	145	JNA 601N	162	KBU 897P
111	HNE 635N	129	JNA 585N	146	JNA 602N	163	KBU 898P
112	HNE 636N	130	JNA 586N	147	JNA 603N	164	KBU 899P
113	HNE 637N	131	JNA 587N	148	JND 991N	165	KBU 900P
114	HNE 638N	132	JNA 588N	149	JND 998N	166	KBU 901P
115	HNE 639N	133	JNA 589N	150	JND 999N	167	KBU 902P
116	HNE 646N	134	JNA 590N	151	JDB 103N	169	KBU 904P
117	HNE 647N	135	JNA 591N	152	KBU 889P	170	KBU 905P
118	HNE 648N						

171-250

Chassis and Body: Leyland National 11351A/1R integral-construction vehicles with B49F bodies, built 1977-1979
206-250 were ex Lancashire United Transport Nos. 465-479/530-536/543-565 in 1981

171	RBU 171R	176	RBU 176R	181	RBU 181R	186	ABA 11T
172	RBU 172R	177	RBU 177R	182	RBU 182R	187	ABA 12T
173	RBU 173R	178	RBU 178R	183	RBU 183R	188	ABA 13T
174	RBU 174R	179	RBU 179R	184	RBU 184R	189	ABA 14T
175	RBU 175R	180	RBU 180R	185	RBU 185R	190	ABA 15T

191	ABA 16T	206	NEN 952R	221	PTD 667S	236	WBN 470T
192	ABA 17T	207	NEN 953R	222	PTD 668S	237	WBN 471T
193	ABA 18T	208	NEN 954R	223	PTD 669S	238	WBN 472T
194	ABA 19T	209	NEN 955R	224	PTD 670S	239	WBN 473T
195	ABA 20T	210	NEN 956R	225	PTD 671S	240	WBN 474T
196	ABA 21T	211	NEN 957R	226	PTD 672S	241	WBN 475T
197	ABA 22T	212	NEN 958R	227	PTD 673S	242	WBN 476T
198	ABA 23T	213	NEN 959R	228	WBN 462T	243	WBN 477T
199	ABA 24T	214	NEN 960R	229	WBN 463T	244	WBN 478T
200	ABA 25T	215	NEN 961R	230	WBN 464T	245	WBN 479T
201	ABA 26T	216	NEN 962R	231	WBN 465T	246	WBN 480T
202	ABA 27T	217	NEN 963R	232	WBN 466T	247	WBN 481T
203	ABA 28T	218	NEN 964R	233	WBN 467T	248	WBN 482T
204	ABA 29T	219	NEN 965R	234	WBN 468T	249	WBN 483T
205	ABA 30T	220	NEN 966R	235	WBN 469T	250	WBN 484T

291-301

Chassis: Bristol RESL6G built 1968
Body: Marshall B43F
Ex North Western Road Car Co Nos. 291-301 in 1972

291	KJA 291G	299	KJA 299G	301	KJA 301G

317-338

Chassis: Bristol RELL6G built 1969
Body: Alexander B48F
Ex North Western Road Car Co Nos. 317-338 in 1972

317	NJA 317H	319	NJA 319H	337	NJA 337H	338	NJA 338H

354-384

Chassis: Seddon 'Pennine' RU built 1970/1971
Body: Plaxton B40D
Ex Lancashire United Transport Nos. 354/369/379/384 in 1981

354	WTD 675H	369	DTC 717J	379	DTC 727J	384	DTC 732J

414-423

Chassis: Bristol RESL6G built 1974
Body: Plaxton DP41F
Ex Lancashire United Transport Nos. 414-423 in 1981

414	TTB 445M	417	TTB 448M	420	TTB 451M	422	TTB 453M
415	TTB 446M	418	TTB 449M	421	TTB 452M	423	TTB 454M
416	TTB 447M	419	VTC 733M				

424

Chassis: Leyland 'Leopard' PSU3C/2R built 1974
Body: Northern Counties DP44F
Ex Lancashire United Transport No. 424 in 1981

424	GBN 331N

430-431

Chassis: Leyland 'Leopard' PSU3C/4R built 1975
Body: Plaxton B44D
Ex Lancashire United Transport Nos. 430/431 in 1981

430	JDK 921P	431	JDK 922P

432-434

Chassis: Leyland 'Leopard' PSU4C/4R built 1975
Body: Plaxton B44F
Ex Lancashire United Transport Nos. 432-434 in 1981

432	JDK 923P	433	JDK 924P	434	JDK 925P

435-464

Chassis: Leyland 'Leopard' PSU3D/2R built 1976
Body: Plaxton B48F
Ex Lancashire United Transport Nos. 435-464 in 1981

LUT's coach fleet transferred to the PTE consisted mainly of Leyland 'Leopards' with Plaxton bodies. Some of the older ones have been repainted and transferred to work on the Manchester Airport express coach route, like 36 (OTD 825R), seen in Portland Street, in Manchester city centre. (D AKRIGG)

LUT also adopted the Leyland/Plaxton combination for more workaday members of the fleet. 446 (MTE 14R) is a Leopard with Plaxton 'Derwent' bus bodywork, seen in Mesnes Street, Wigan, under PTE ownership. LUT bought many batches of buses bodied by the Scarborough firm. (A M WITTON)

The Bristol VR with ECW bodywork is common in most other parts of England and Wales; but in Greater Manchester, apart from outside visitors from NBC fleets there are only 25 owned by the PTE. They came as a result of a North Western order and were delivered to the SELNEC Cheshire company; all have spent their entire working lives at Stockport garage. 1422 (AJA 122L) is seen in the Stockport bus station. (D AKRIGG)

The three views on this page demonstrate PTE's propensity to buy all manner of experimental buses to vary the usual diet of Atlanteans, Fleetlines, Metrobuses and Nationals. Dennis 'Dominator' 1422 (TND 440X), one of four, is allocated to Oldham garage. It is seen in Yorkshire Street, Oldham, of which this part has recently been converted to a pedestrian and bus only lane. (A M WITTON)

Stockport's long-serving Leyland PD3s were not even withdrawn when a new front-engined double-decker arrived in the town. Ailsa-Volvo 1446 (NNA 134W) features a front entrance but up to now it has been used only on two man operated services such as 207 and 330. It is arriving in Stockport's Mersey Square from Ashton on the latter route. (A M WITTON)

Likely to lead to a more permanent answer to the PTE's vehicle supply problem, the experimental Leyland 'Olympian' has already led to a quantity order for the type. 1451 (NJA 568W) was seen crossing Cheetham Hill Road railway bridge en route to Shaw on the long 59 route. It was fitted with an electronic dot matrix destination display, which has since been replaced by more conventional equipment. (A M WITTON)

er half of the 400-d 'Mancunians' designed by Manchester City ansport are still traffic with the E, although the number shrinking almost ery week. One of the st, 2300 (SVR 300K) s seen in Victoria reet, Manchester, ssing the fine fifteenth century Cathedral. e easiest way to distinguish a 'Mancunian' the distance is that e route number blind on the offside, not arside. (A M WITTON)

Since 1974 the Wigan fleet has been reduced to two batches of Leyland Atlanteans with Northern Counties bodywork. 3337 (NEK 8K) was of the last Wigan batch, given corresponding fleet numbers which were to have been the start of a new and more logical numbering system! Station Road in Wigan is the scene. (D AKRIGG)

reater Manchester's 5 TN-type Titans are ivided between Birchields Road, Oldham nd Stockport garages, ive buses at each. ldham's share includes 006 (GNF 6V), photographed near the foot of orkshire Street. (A WITTON)

The annual Trans-Lan[cs] bus rally, culminati[ng] in a display at Heat[on] Park, affords an oppor[t]unity to see the late[st] models cheek by jo[wl] with venerable vehicl[es] of yesteryear. The la[t]est Metrobuses for t[he] PTE fleet include 51[69] (ANA 169Y), seen ne[xt] to a new-type 'Standar[d'] 8535 (ANA 535Y), bo[th] wearing the PTE's ne[w] style livery.
(A M WITTON)

The Metrobus series has constantly been chasing, but never quite caught up with, the 5100 series of double-deckers acquired from the Oldham undertaking. The last Oldham-type vehicles will soon be gone, so solving the administrative problem. 5197 (ABU 197J) is a Roe-bodied Atlantean delivered to the PTE against Oldham's last orders as an independent undertaking. It was seen in Mumps bus station, Oldham.(A M WITTON)

The last LUT doubl[e] deckers, by contras[t] were indistinguishab[le] from PTE 'standard['] except as regards live[ry] and fleetname, and so[on] even those distinctio[ns] will have disappeare[d]. The last of all, 69[06] (DWH 706W) is seen [in] Bolton bus station [on] route 12, which in 'mu[n]icipal' days was worke[d] jointly by LUT, Bolt[on] and Salford Corpora[t]ions. (A M WITTON)

435	LTE 486P	443	LTE 494P	451	MTE 19R	458	MTE 26R
436	LTE 487P	444	LTE 495P	452	MTE 20R	459	MTE 27R
437	LTE 488P	445	MTE 13R	453	MTE 21R	460	MTE 28R
438	LTE 489P	446	MTE 14R	454	MTE 22R	461	MTE 29R
439	LTE 490P	447	MTE 15R	455	MTE 23R	462	MTE 30R
440	LTE 491P	448	MTE 16R	456	MTE 24R	463	MTE 31R
441	LTE 492P	449	MTE 17R	457	MTE 25R	464	MTE 32R
442	LTE 493P	450	MTE 18R				

1024

Chassis: Leyland 'Atlantean' PDR1/1 built 1968
Body: Park Royal H45/28D
Ex Manchester Corporation No. 1024 in 1969

1024   HVM 924F

1079-1219

Chassis: Leyland 'Atlantean' PDR2/1 built 1968-1970
Body: (1079) Park Royal H47/29D
(1106-1126/1161-1192) Park Royal H47/28D
(1142-1151) East Lancs H47/26D
(1204-1219) Metro-Cammell H47/30D

1079 was ex Manchester Corporation No. 1079 in 1969
1106-1192 were ordered by Manchester Corporation
1204-1219 were ordered by Salford Corporation

1079	LNA 179G	1142	NNB 547H	1170	ONF 858H	1187	ONF 875H
1106	NNB 515H	1144	NNB 549H	1171	ONF 859H	1188	ONF 876H
1108	NNB 517H	1146	NNB 551H	1172	ONF 860H	1189	ONF 877H
1111	NNB 520H	1148	NNB 553H	1173	ONF 861H	1190	ONF 878H
1112	NNB 521H	1149	NNB 554H	1174	ONF 862H	1191	ONF 879H
1113	NNB 522H	1150	NNB 555H	1175	ONF 863H	1192	ONF 880H
1115	NNB 524H	1151	NNB 556H	1176	ONF 864H	1204	SRJ 327H
1118	NNB 527H	1161	ONF 849H	1177	ONF 865H	1206	SRJ 329H
1119	NNB 528H	1162	ONF 850H	1178	ONF 866H	1207	SRJ 330H
1120	NNB 529H	1163	ONF 851H	1179	ONF 867H	1211	SRJ 334H
1121	NNB 530H	1164	ONF 852H	1180	ONF 868H	1212	SRJ 335H
1122	NNB 531H	1165	ONF 853H	1182	ONF 870H	1214	SRJ 337H
1123	NNB 532H	1166	ONF 854H	1183	ONF 871H	1215	SRJ 338H
1124	NNB 533H	1167	ONF 855H	1184	ONF 872H	1216	SRJ 339H
1125	NNB 534H	1168	ONF 856H	1185	ONF 873H	1218	SRJ 341H
1126	NNB 535H	1169	ONF 857H	1186	ONF 874H	1219	SRJ 342H

1300-1319

Chassis and Body: Leyland National 1051/1R integral construction vehicles with B41F bodies, built 1974/1975

1300	XVU 367M	1305	XVU 372M	1310	XVU 377M	1316	XVU 383M
1301	XVU 368M	1306	XVU 373M	1311	XVU 378M	1317	XVU 384M
1302	XVU 369M	1307	XVU 374M	1312	XVU 379M	1318	XVU 385M
1303	XVU 370M	1308	XVU 375M	1313	XVU 380M	1319	GND 511N
1304	XVU 371M	1309	XVU 376M	1315	XVU 382M		

1330-1337

Chassis and Body: Leyland National 1151/2R integral construction vehicles with B45D bodies (1330 is B43D), built 1972

1330	TXJ 507K	1332	TXJ 509K	1334	TXJ 511K	1336	TXJ 513K
1331	TXJ 508K	1333	TXJ 510K	1335	TXJ 512K	1337	TXJ 514K

1338-1341

Chassis and Body: Leyland National 1051/2R integral construction vehicles with B39D bodies, built 1973

1338	VVM 601L	1339	VVM 602L	1340	VVM 603L	1341	VVM 604L

1342-1349

Chassis: Scania BR111MH built 1972
Body: Metro-Cammell B44D

1342	TXJ 515K	1346	TXJ 519K	1348	TXJ 521K	1349	TXJ 522K
1343	TXJ 516K						

1351-1360

Chassis: Scania BR110MH built 1972/1973
Body: Metro-Cammell B40D

1351	VVM 606L	1352	VVM 607L	1353	VVM 608L	1360	VVM 609L

1400-1424

Chassis: Bristol VRTSL6G built 1973
Body: ECW H43/32F
Ordered by North Western Road Car Co

1400	AJA 400L	1407	AJA 407L	1413	AJA 413L	1419	AJA 419L
1401	AJA 401L	1408	AJA 408L	1414	AJA 414L	1420	AJA 420L
1402	AJA 402L	1409	AJA 409L	1415	AJA 415L	1421	AJA 421L
1403	AJA 403L	1410	AJA 410L	1416	AJA 416L	1422	AJA 422L
1404	AJA 404L	1411	AJA 411L	1417	AJA 417L	1423	AJA 423L
1405	AJA 405L	1412	AJA 412L	1418	AJA 418L	1424	AJA 424L
1406	AJA 406L						

1437-1438

Chassis: Dennis 'Dominator' DD110 built 1980
Body: Northern Counties H43/32F

		1437	HDB 437V	1438	HDB 438V		

1439-1440

Chassis: Dennis 'Dominator' DDA136 built 1981
Body: Northern Counties H43/32F

		1439	TND 439X	1440	TND 440X	1441	

1446-1448

Chassis: Volvo-Ailsa AB55-10 Mk II built 1980/1982
Body: Northern Counties H44/35F

	1446	NNA 134W	1447	WRJ 447X	1448	WRJ 448X

1451

Chassis: Leyland 'Olympian' B45-TL11-1R built 1980
Body: Northern Counties H43/30F

1451   NJA 568W

1715-1742

Chassis: Seddon 'Pennine' IV/236 built 1974/1975
Body: Seddon B19F

1715	XVU 345M	1721	XVU 351M	1728	XVU 358M	1734	XVU 364M
1716	XVU 346M	1722	XVU 352M	1729	XVU 359M	1738	HJA 122N
1717	XVU 347M	1723	XVU 353M	1730	XVU 360M	1739	HJA 123N
1718	XVU 348M	1724	XVU 354M	1731	XVU 361M	1740	HJA 124N
1719	XVU 349M	1726	XVU 356M	1732	XVU 362M	1741	HJA 125N
1720	XVU 350M	1727	XVU 357M	1733	XVU 363M	1742	HJA 126N

2104-2304

Chassis: Daimler 'Fleetline' CRG6LXB-33 built 1970-1972
Body: (2104-2144/2211-2270) Park Royal H47/28D
         (2151-2209) Metro-Cammell H47/29D
         (2271-2304) Roe H47/29D
Ordered by Manchester Corporation

2104	NNB 563H	2110	NNB 569H	2117	NNB 576H	2122	NNB 581H
2106	NNB 565H	2114	NNB 573H	2121	NNB 578H	2123	NNB 582H
2108	NNB 567H	2116	NNB 575H	2121	NNB 580H	2124	NNB 583H

2125	NNB 584H	2180	PNA 219J	2222	RNA 222J	2265	RNA 265J
2126	NNB 585H	2181	PNA 220J	2223	RNA 223J	2266	RNA 266J
2128	NNB 587H	2182	PNA 221J	2224	RNA 224J	2267	RNA 267J
2129	NNB 588H	2183	PNA 222J	2226	RNA 226J	2268	RNA 268J
2130	NNB 589H	2184	PNA 223J	2227	RNA 227J	2269	RNA 269J
2131	NNB 590H	2185	PNA 224J	2228	RNA 228J	2270	RNA 270J
2132	NNB 591H	2186	PNA 225J	2229	RNA 229J	2271	SVR 271J
2133	NNB 592H	2187	PNA 226J	2231	RNA 231J	2272	SVR 272K
2134	NNB 593H	2188	PNA 227J	2232	RNA 232J	2273	SVR 273K
2135	NNB 594H	2189	PNA 228J	2234	RNA 234J	2274	SVR 274K
2136	NNB 595H	2190	PNA 229J	2235	RNA 235J	2275	SVR 275K
2137	NNB 596H	2191	PNA 230J	2236	RNA 236J	2276	SVR 276K
2138	NNB 597H	2192	PNA 231J	2237	RNA 237J	2277	SVR 277K
2139	NNB 598H	2193	PNA 232J	2238	RNA 238J	2278	SVR 278K
2140	NNB 599H	2194	PNA 233J	2239	RNA 239J	2279	SVR 279K
2142	NNB 601H	2195	PNA 234J	2240	RNA 240J	2280	SVR 280K
2144	NNB 603H	2197	PNA 236J	2241	RNA 241J	2281	SVR 281K
2151	ONF 883H	2198	PNA 237J	2242	RNA 242J	2282	SVR 282K
2152	ONF 884H	2199	PNA 238J	2243	RNA 243J	2283	SVR 283K
2155	ONF 887H	2200	PNA 239J	2244	RNA 244J	2284	SVR 284K
2156	ONF 888H	2201	PNA 240J	2245	RNA 245J	2285	SVR 285K
2157	ONF 889H	2202	PNA 241J	2246	RNA 246J	2286	SVR 286K
2158	ONF 890H	2203	PNA 242J	2247	RNA 247J	2287	SVR 287K
2160	ONF 892H	2204	PNA 243J	2248	RNA 248J	2288	SVR 288K
2162	PNA 201J	2205	PNA 244J	2249	RNA 249J	2289	SVR 289K
2163	PNA 202J	2206	PNA 245J	2250	RNA 250J	2290	SVR 290K
2164	PNA 203J	2207	PNA 246J	2251	RNA 251J	2291	SVR 291K
2165	PNA 204J	2208	PNA 247J	2252	RNA 252J	2292	SVR 292K
2166	PNA 205J	2209	PNA 248J	2253	RNA 253J	2293	SVR 293K
2167	PNA 206J	2211	RNA 211J	2254	RNA 254J	2294	SVR 294K
2168	PNA 207J	2212	RNA 212J	2255	RNA 255J	2295	SVR 295K
2169	PNA 208J	2213	RNA 213J	2256	RNA 256J	2296	SVR 296K
2170	PNA 209J	2214	RNA 214J	2257	RNA 257J	2297	SVR 297K
2171	PNA 210J	2215	RNA 215J	2258	RNA 258J	2298	SVR 298K
2172	PNA 211J	2216	RNA 216J	2259	RNA 259J	2299	SVR 299K
2173	PNA 212J	2217	RNA 217J	2260	RNA 260J	2300	SVR 300K
2174	PNA 213J	2218	RNA 218J	2261	RNA 261J	2301	SVR 301K
2175	PNA 214J	2219	RNA 219J	2262	RNA 262J	2302	SVR 302K
2177	PNA 216J	2220	RNA 220J	2263	RNA 263J	2303	SVR 303K
2178	PNA 217J	2221	RNA 221J	2264	RNA 264J	2304	SVR 304K
2179	PNA 218J						

2318-2337 Chassis: Daimler 'Fleetline' CRL6 built 1972/1973
Body: (2327/2330/2332-2337)Metro-Cammell H44/27F
(2318-2326/2328/2329/2331) Park Royal H44/27F

Ex Lancashire United Transport Nos. 318-337 in 1981; acquired by them from London Transport Nos. DMS597/584/588/591/603/615/622/634/635/1407/632/675/1489/710/1452/1458/1460/1462/1465/1466 respectively in 1980

2318	MLK 597L	2323	MLK 615L	2328	MLK 632L	2333	MLH 458L
2319	MLK 584L	2324	MLK 622L	2329	MLK 675L	2334	MLH 460L
2320	MLK 588L	2325	MLK 634L	2330	MLH 489L	2335	MLH 462L
2321	MLK 591L	2326	MLK 635L	2331	TGX 710M	2336	MLH 465L
2322	MLK 603L	2327	MLH 407L	2332	MLH 452L	2337	MLH 466L

2358-2413

Chassis: Daimler 'Fleetline' CRG6LXB built 1970-1974
Body: Northern Counties H49/27D (2394/2398-2400/2403 are H47/32F)
Ex Lancashire United Transport Nos. 358-363/394-413 in 1981
2413 is being rebodied by Northern Counties to single-doorway layout after accident damage. The new seating capacity is not yet known

2358	ATJ 272J	2395	RTJ 423L	2402	RTJ 430L	2408	VTC 498M
2359	ATJ 273J	2396	RTJ 424L	2403	RTJ 431L	2409	VTC 499M
2360	ATJ 274J	2397	RTJ 425L	2404	VTC 494M	2410	VTC 500M
2361	ATJ 275J	2398	RTJ 426L	2405	VTC 495M	2411	VTC 501M
2362	ATJ 276J	2399	RTJ 427L	2406	VTC 496M	2412	VTC 502M
2363	ATJ 277J	2400	RTJ 428L	2407	VTC 497M	2413	VTC 503M
2394	RTJ 422L	2401	RTJ 429L				

3001-3015

Chassis: Leyland 'Olympian' ONTL11/1R on order 1982
Body: Northern Counties H / F

3001	ANA 1Y	3005	ANA 5Y	3009	ANA 9Y	3013	ANA 13Y
3002	ANA 2Y	3006	ANA 6Y	3010	ANA 10Y	3014	ANA 14Y
3003	ANA 3Y	3007	ANA 7Y	3011	ANA 11Y	3015	ANA 15Y
3004	ANA 4Y	3008	ANA 8Y	3012	ANA 12Y		

3016-3025

Chassis: Leyland 'Olympian' ONLXB/1R on order 1982
Body: Northern Counties H / F

3016	ANA 16Y	3019	ANA 19Y	3022	ANA 22Y	3024	ANA 24Y
3017	ANA 17Y	3020	ANA 20Y	3023	ANA 23Y	3025	ANA 25Y
3018	ANA 18Y	3021	ANA 21Y				

3310-3321

Chassis: Leyland 'Atlantean' PDR2/1 built 1972
Body: Northern Counties H48/31D
Ex Wigan Corporation Nos. 92-97, 151-156 in 1974

3310	KJP 20J	3314	KJP 24J	3318	KJP 28J	3320	KJP 30J
3311	KJP 21J	3315	KJP 25J	3319	KJP 29J	3321	KJP 31J
3312	KJP 22J	3316	KJP 26J				

3330-3339

Chassis: Leyland 'Atlantean' AN68/2R built 1972
Body: Northern Counties H48/31D
Ex Wigan Corporation Nos. 1-10 in 1974

3330	NEK 1K	3333	NEK 4K	3336	NEK 7K	3338	NEK 9K
3331	NEK 2K	3334	NEK 5K	3337	NEK 8K	3339	NEK 10K
3332	NEK 3K	3335	NEK 6K				

4001-4015

Chassis: Leyland 'Titan' TNLXB/1RF (4012-4015 are TNTL11/1RF) built 1978-1980
Body: Park Royal H46/27F (4001/4006/4007 are H47/26F)

4001	ANE 1T	4005	ANE 5T	4009	GNF 9V	4013	GNF 13V
4002	ANE 2T	4006	GNF 6V	4010	GNF 10V	4014	GNF 14V
4003	FVR 3V	4007	GNF 7V	4011	GNF 11V	4015	GNF 15V
4004	ANE 4T	4008	GNF 8V	4012	GNF 12V		

5001-5010

Chassis: MCW 'Metrobus' DR101/6 built 1979
Body: Metro-Cammell H43/30F

5001	GBU 1V	5004	GBU 4V	5007	GBU 7V	5009	GBU 9V
5002	GBU 2V	5005	GBU 5V	5008	GBU 8V	5010	GBU 10V
5003	GBU 3V	5006	GBU 6V				

5011-5030

Chassis: MCW 'Metrobus' DR102/10 built 1980
Body: Metro-Cammell H43/30F

5011	GBU 11V	5016	GBU 16V	5021	MNC 496W	5026	MNC 498W
5012	GBU 12V	5017	GBU 17V	5022	GBU 22V	5027	GBU 27V
5013	GBU 13V	5018	MNC 494W	5023	MNC 497W	5028	GBU 28V
5014	GBU 14V	5019	MNC 495W	5024	GBU 24V	5029	GBU 29V
5015	GBU 15V	5020	GBU 20V	5025	GBU 25V	5030	MNC 499W

5031-5110

Chassis: MCW 'Metrobus' DR102/21 built 1980/1981
Body: Metro-Cammell H43/30F

5031	MRJ 31W	5051	MRJ 51W	5071	ORJ 71W	5091	ORJ 91W
5032	MRJ 32W	5052	MRJ 52W	5072	ORJ 72W	5092	ORJ 92W
5033	MRJ 33W	5053	MRJ 53W	5073	ORJ 73W	5093	ORJ 93W
5034	MRJ 34W	5054	MRJ 54W	5074	ORJ 74W	5094	ORJ 94W
5035	MRJ 35W	5055	MRJ 55W	5075	ORJ 75W	5095	ORJ 95W
5036	MRJ 36W	5056	MRJ 56W	5076	ORJ 76W	5096	ORJ 96W
5037	MRJ 37W	5057	MRJ 57W	5077	ORJ 77W	5097	ORJ 97W
5038	MRJ 38W	5058	MRJ 58W	5078	ORJ 78W	5098	ORJ 98W
5039	MRJ 39W	5059	MRJ 59W	5079	ORJ 79W	5099	ORJ 99W
5040	MRJ 40W	5060	MRJ 60W	5080	ORJ 80W	5100	ORJ 100W
5041	MRJ 41W	5061	MRJ 61W	5081	ORJ 81W	5101	SND 101X
5042	MRJ 42W	5062	MRJ 62W	5082	ORJ 82W	5102	SND 102X
5043	MRJ 43W	5063	MRJ 63W	5083	ORJ 83W	5103	SND 103X
5044	MRJ 44W	5064	MRJ 64W	5084	ORJ 84W	5104	SND 104X
5045	MRJ 45W	5065	MRJ 65W	5085	ORJ 85W	5105	SND 105X
5046	MRJ 46W	5066	MRJ 66W	5086	ORJ 86W	5106	SND 106X
5047	MRJ 47W	5067	MRJ 67W	5087	ORJ 87W	5107	SND 107X
5048	MRJ 48W	5068	MRJ 68W	5088	ORJ 88W	5108	SND 108X
5049	MRJ 49W	5069	MRJ 69W	5089	ORJ 89W	5109	SND 109X
5050	MRJ 50W	5070	MRJ 70W	5090	ORJ 90W	5110	SND 110X

5111-5190

Chassis: MCW 'Metrobus' DR102/23 built 1981/1982 and on order
Body: Metro-Cammell H43/30F

5111	SND 111X	5129	SND 129X	5147	SND 147X	5165	ANA 165Y
5112	SND 112X	5130	SND 130X	5148	SND 148X	5166	ANA 166Y
5113	SND 113X	5131	SND 131X	5149	SND 149X	5167	ANA 167Y
5114	SND 114X	5132	SND 132X	5150	SND 150X	5168	ANA 168Y
5115	SND 115X	5133	SND 133X	5151	ANA 151Y	5169	ANA 169Y
5116	SND 116X	5134	SND 134X	5152	ANA 152Y	5170	ANA 170Y
5117	SND 117X	5135	SND 135X	5153	ANA 153Y	5171	
5118	SND 118X	5136	SND 136X	5154	ANA 154Y	5172	
5119	SND 119X	5137	SND 137X	5155	ANA 155Y	5173	
5120	SND 120X	5138	SND 138X	5156	ANA 156Y	5174	
5121	SND 121X	5139	SND 139X	5157	ANA 157Y	5175	
5122	SND 122X	5140	SND 140X	5158	ANA 158Y	5176	
5123	SND 123X	5141	SND 141X	5159	ANA 159Y	5177	
5124	SND 124X	5142	SND 142X	5160	ANA 160Y	5178	
5125	SND 125X	5143	SND 143X	5161	ANA 161Y	5179	
5126	SND 126X	5144	SND 144X	5162	ANA 162Y	5180	
5127	SND 127X	5145	SND 145X	5163	ANA 163Y	5181	
5128	SND 128X	5146	SND 146X	5164	ANA 164Y	5182	

| 5183 | 5185 | 5187 | 5189 |
| 5184 | 5186 | 5188 | 5190 |

5191-5199

Chassis: Leyland 'Atlantean' PDR1A/1 built 1971
Body: Roe H43/31D
Ordered by Oldham Corporation

| 5191 | ABU 191J | 5193 | ABU 193J | 5196 | ABU 196J | 5199 | ABU 199J |
| 5192 | ABU 192J | 5194 | ABU 194J | 5197 | ABU 197J | 5198 | |

5466-5471

Chassis: Leyland 'Atlantean' PDR1A/1 built 1971
Body: Northern Counties H43/32F
Ordered by Ashton-under-Lyne Corporation; delivered as EX1-EX6, the first prototypes of the standard SELNEC double-deck bus

| 5466 | PNF 941J | 5468 | PNF 943J | 5470 | PNF 945J | 5471 | PNF 946J |
| 5467 | PNF 942J | 5469 | PNF 944J | | | | |

6245-6254

Chassis: Daimler 'Fleetline' CRG6LXB built 1972
Body: (6245-6249) Northern Counties H43/32F
         (6250-6254) Northern Counties H45/27D
Ordered by Rochdale Corporation; delivered as prototype 'standards' Nos. EX7-11, EX17-21

6245	TNB 747K	6248	TNB 750K	6251	TNB 758K	6253	TNB 760K
6246	TNB 748K	6249	TNB 751K	6252	TNB 759K	6254	TNB 761K
6247	TNB 749K	6250	TNB 757K				

6346-6350

Chassis: Daimler 'Fleetline' CRG6LX built 1970
Body: East Lancs H45/28D
Ordered by Bury Corporation

| 6346 | NEN 506J | 6347 | NEN 507J | 6349 | NEN 509J | 6350 | NEN 510J |

6395-6399

Chassis: Daimler 'Fleetline' CRG6LXB built 1972
Body: Northern Counties H43/32F
Ordered by Bury Corporation; delivered as prototype 'standards' Nos. EX12-16

| 6395 | TNB 752K | 6397 | TNB 754K | 6398 | TNB 755K | 6399 | TNB 756K |
| 6396 | TNB 753K | | | | | | |

6798-6801

Chassis: Leyland 'Atlantean' PDR1A/1 built 1969/1970
Body: East Lancs H43/27D
Ordered by Bolton Corporation

| 6798 | OBN 298H | 6800 | OBN 300H | 6801 | OBN 301H |

6802-6816

Chassis: Leyland 'Atlantean' PDR2/1 built 1972
Body: East Lancs H49/37F
Ordered by Bolton Corporation

6802	TWH 802K	6806	TWH 806K	6810	TWH 810K	6814	TWH 814K
6803	TWH 803K	6807	TWH 807K	6811	TWH 811K	6815	TWH 815K
6804	TWH 804K	6808	TWH 808K	6812	TWH 812K	6816	TWH 816K
6805	TWH 805K	6809	TWH 809K	6813	TWH 813K		

6901-6940

Chassis: Daimler 'Fleetline' FE30AGR built 1977-1979
Body: Northern Counties H43/32F (6912 is being fitted with a new Northern Counties H43/32F body in 1982 following accident damage)
Ex Lancashire United Transport Nos. 485-524 in 1981

6901	OBN 502R	6911	PTD 639S	6921	PTD 649S	6931	TWH 690T
6902	OBN 503R	6912	PTD 640S	6922	PTD 650S	6932	TWH 691T
6903	OBN 504R	6913	PTD 641S	6923	PTD 651S	6933	TWH 692T
6904	OBN 505R	6914	PTD 642S	6924	PTD 652S	6934	TWH 693T
6905	OBN 506R	6915	PTD 643S	6925	PTD 653S	6935	TWH 694T
6906	OBN 507R	6916	PTD 644S	6926	PTD 654S	6936	TWH 695T
6907	OBN 508R	6917	PTD 645S	6927	PTD 655S	6937	TWH 696T
6908	OBN 509R	6918	PTD 646S	6928	PTD 656S	6938	TWH 697T
6909	OBN 510R	6919	PTD 647S	6929	PTD 657S	6939	TWH 698T
6910	OBN 511R	6920	PTD 648S	6930	PTD 658S	6940	TWH 699T

6941-6990

Chassis: Leyland 'Fleetline' FE30AGR built 1979/1980
Body: Northern Counties H43/32F
Ex Lancashire United Transport Nos. 525-529, 542, 570-613 in 1981

6941	TWH 700T	6954	YTE 591V	6967	DWH 683W	6979	DWH 695W
6942	TWH 701T	6955	YTE 592V	6968	DWH 684W	6980	DWH 696W
6943	TWH 702T	6956	YTE 593V	6969	DWH 685W	6981	DWH 697W
6944	TWH 703T	6957	BCB 610V	6970	DWH 686W	6982	DWH 698W
6945	TWH 704T	6958	BCB 611V	6971	DWH 687W	6983	DWH 699W
6946	WWH 94T	6959	BCB 612V	6972	DWH 688W	6984	DWH 700W
6947	YTE 584V	6960	BCB 613V	6973	DWH 689W	6985	DWH 701W
6948	YTE 585V	6961	BCB 614V	6974	DWH 690W	6986	DWH 702W
6949	YTE 586V	6962	BCB 615V	6975	DWH 691W	6987	DWH 703W
6950	YTE 587V	6963	BCB 616V	6976	DWH 692W	6988	DWH 704W
6951	YTE 588V	6964	BCB 617V	6977	DWH 693W	6989	DWH 705W
6952	YTE 589V	6965	BCB 618V	6978	DWH 694W	6990	DWH 706W
6953	YTE 590V	6966	DWH 682W				

7001-7150

Chassis: Leyland 'Atlantean' AN68/1R built 1972/1973
Body: (7001-7031/7033-7145) Park Royal H43/32F
(7032) Park Royal O43/32F
(7146-7150) Northern Counties H43/32F

7001	VNB 101L	7017	VNB 117L	7033	VNB 133L	7049	VNB 149L
7002	VNB 102L	7018	VNB 118L	7034	VNB 134L	7050	VNB 150L
7003	VNB 103L	7019	VNB 119L	7035	VNB 135L	7051	VNB 151L
7004	VNB 104L	7020	VNB 120L	7036	VNB 136L	7052	VNB 152L
7005	VNB 105L	7021	VNB 121L	7037	VNB 137L	7053	VNB 153L
7006	VNB 106L	7022	VNB 122L	7038	VNB 138L	7054	VNB 154L
7007	VNB 107L	7023	VNB 123L	7039	VNB 139L	7055	VNB 155L
7008	VNB 108L	7024	VNB 124L	7040	VNB 140L	7056	VNB 156L
7009	VNB 109L	7025	VNB 125L	7041	VNB 141L	7057	VNB 157L
7010	VNB 110L	7026	VNB 126L	7042	VNB 142L	7058	VNB 158L
7011	VNB 111L	7027	VNB 127L	7043	VNB 143L	7059	VNB 159L
7012	VNB 112L	7028	VNB 128L	7044	VNB 144L	7060	VNB 160L
7013	VNB 113L	7029	VNB 129L	7045	VNB 145L	7061	VNB 161L
7014	VNB 114L	7030	VNB 130L	7046	VNB 146L	7062	VNB 162L
7015	VNB 115L	7031	VNB 131L	7047	VNB 147L	7063	VNB 163L
7016	VNB 116L	7032	VNB 132L	7048	VNB 148L	7064	VNB 164L

7065	VNB 165L	7087	WBN 965L	7109	WBN 987L	7130	XJA 521L
7066	VNB 166L	7088	WBN 966L	7110	XJA 501L	7131	XJA 522L
7067	VNB 167L	7089	WBN 967L	7111	XJA 502L	7132	XJA 523L
7068	VNB 168L	7090	WBN 968L	7112	XJA 503L	7133	XJA 524L
7069	VNB 169L	7091	WBN 969L	7113	XJA 504L	7134	XJA 525L
7070	VNB 170L	7092	WBN 970L	7114	XJA 505L	7135	XJA 526L
7071	VNB 171L	7093	WBN 971L	7115	XJA 506L	7136	XJA 527L
7072	WBN 950L	7094	WBN 972L	7116	XJA 507L	7137	XJA 528L
7073	WBN 951L	7095	WBN 973L	7117	XJA 508L	7138	XJA 529L
7074	WBN 952L	7096	WBN 974L	7118	XJA 509L	7139	XJA 530L
7075	WBN 953L	7097	WBN 975L	7119	XJA 510L	7140	XJA 531L
7076	WBN 954L	7098	WBN 976L	7120	XJA 511L	7141	XJA 532L
7077	WBN 955L	7099	WBN 977L	7121	XJA 512L	7142	XJA 533L
7078	WBN 956L	7100	WBN 978L	7122	XJA 513L	7143	XJA 534L
7079	WBN 957L	7101	WBN 979L	7123	XJA 514L	7144	XJA 535L
7080	WBN 958L	7102	WBN 980L	7124	XJA 515L	7145	XJA 536L
7081	WBN 959L	7103	WBN 981L	7125	XJA 516L	7146	VNB 172L
7082	WBN 960L	7104	WBN 982L	7126	XJA 517L	7147	VNB 173L
7083	WBN 961L	7105	WBN 983L	7127	XJA 518L	7148	VNB 174L
7084	WBN 962L	7106	WBN 984L	7128	XJA 519L	7149	VNB 175L
7085	WBN 963L	7107	WBN 985L	7129	XJA 520L	7150	VNB 176L
7086	WBN 964L	7108	WBN 986L				

7151-7500 Chassis: Daimler 'Fleetline' CRG6LXB built 1972-1976
Body: (7151-7205) Park Royal H43/32F
(7206-7251/7280/7281) Northern Counties H45/27D
(7252-7279/7282-7500) Northern Counties H43/32F

7151	WBN 988L	7179	WWH 37L	7207	VNB 178L	7235	VNB 206L
7152	WBN 989L	7180	WWH 38L	7208	VNB 179L	7236	VNB 207L
7153	WBN 990L	7181	WWH 39L	7209	VNB 180L	7237	VNB 208L
7154	WBN 991L	7182	WWH 40L	7210	VNB 181L	7238	VNB 209L
7155	WBN 992L	7183	WWH 41L	7211	VNB 182L	7239	VNB 210L
7156	WBN 993L	7184	WWH 42L	7212	VNB 183L	7240	VNB 211L
7157	WBN 994L	7185	WWH 43L	7213	VNB 184L	7241	VNB 212L
7158	WBN 995L	7186	WWH 44L	7214	VNB 185L	7242	VNB 213L
7159	WBN 996L	7187	XJA 537L	7215	VNB 186L	7243	VNB 214L
7160	WBN 997L	7188	XJA 538L	7216	VNB 187L	7244	VNB 215L
7161	WBN 998L	7189	XJA 539L	7217	VNB 188L	7245	VNB 216L
7162	WBN 999L	7190	XJA 540L	7218	VNB 189L	7246	VNB 217L
7163	WWH 21L	7191	XJA 541L	7219	VNB 190L	7247	VNB 218L
7164	WWH 22L	7192	XJA 542L	7220	VNB 191L	7248	VNB 219L
7165	WWH 23L	7193	XJA 543L	7221	VNB 192L	7249	VNB 220L
7166	WWH 24L	7194	XJA 544L	7222	VNB 193L	7250	VNB 221L
7167	WWH 25L	7195	XJA 545L	7223	VNB 194L	7251	VNB 222L
7168	WWH 26L	7196	XJA 546L	7224	VNB 195L	7252	VNB 223L
7169	WWH 27L	7197	XJA 547L	7225	VNB 196L	7253	VNB 224L
7170	WWH 28L	7198	XJA 548L	7226	VNB 197L	7254	VNB 225L
7171	WWH 29L	7199	XJA 549L	7227	VNB 198L	7255	VNB 226L
7172	WWH 30L	7200	XJA 550L	7228	VNB 199L	7256	VNB 227L
7173	WWH 31L	7201	XJA 551L	7229	VNB 200L	7257	VNB 228L
7174	WWH 32L	7202	XJA 552L	7230	VNB 201L	7258	VNB 229L
7175	WWH 33L	7203	XJA 553L	7231	VNB 202L	7259	VNB 230L
7176	WWH 34L	7204	XJA 554L	7232	VNB 203L	7260	VNB 231L
7177	WWH 35L	7205	XJA 555L	7233	VNB 204L	7261	VNB 232L
7178	WWH 36L	7206	VNB 177L	7234	VNB 205L	7262	VNB 233L

7263	VNB 234L	7323	XJA 579L	7383	YNA 338M	7442	GND 508N
7264	VNB 235L	7324	XJA 580L	7384	YNA 339M	7443	GDB 162N
7265	VNB 236L	7325	YNA 280M	7385	YNA 340M	7444	GDB 163N
7266	VNB 237L	7326	YNA 281M	7386	YNA 341M	7445	GDB 164N
7267	VNB 238L	7327	YNA 282M	7387	YNA 342M	7446	GDB 165N
7268	VNB 239L	7328	YNA 283M	7388	YNA 343M	7447	GDB 166N
7269	VNB 240L	7329	YNA 284M	7389	YNA 344M	7448	HJA 116N
7270	VNB 241L	7330	YNA 285M	7390	YNA 345M	7449	HJA 117N
7271	YNA 271M	7331	YNA 286M	7391	YNA 346M	7450	HJA 118N
7272	YNA 272M	7332	YNA 287M	7392	YNA 347M	7451	HJA 119N
7273	YNA 273M	7333	YNA 288M	7393	YNA 348M	7452	HJA 120N
7274	YNA 274M	7334	YNA 289M	7394	YNA 349M	7453	JND 981N
7275	YNA 275M	7335	YNA 290M	7395	YNA 350M	7454	JND 982N
7276	YNA 276M	7336	YNA 291M	7396	YNA 351M	7455	JND 983N
7277	YNA 277M	7337	YNA 292M	7397	YNA 352M	7456	JDB 108N
7278	YNA 278M	7338	YNA 293M	7398	YNA 353M	7457	JDB 109N
7279	YNA 279M	7339	YNA 294M	7399	YNA 354M	7458	JDB 110N
7280	WWH 45L	7340	YNA 295M	7400	YNA 355M	7459	JDB 111N
7281	WWH 46L	7341	YNA 296M	7401	YNA 356M	7460	JVM 991N
7282	WWH 47L	7342	YNA 297M	7402	YNA 357M	7461	JVM 992N
7283	WWH 48L	7343	YNA 298M	7403	YNA 358M	7462	JVM 993N
7284	WWH 49L	7344	YNA 299M	7404	YNA 359M	7463	JVM 994N
7285	WWH 50L	7345	YNA 300M	7405	YNA 360M	7464	JVM 995N
7286	WWH 51L	7346	YNA 301M	7406	YNA 361M	7465	KBU 906P
7287	WWH 52L	7347	YNA 302M	7407	YNA 362M	7466	KBU 907P
7288	WWH 53L	7348	YNA 303M	7408	YNA 363M	7467	KBU 908P
7289	WWH 54L	7349	YNA 304M	7409	YNA 364M	7468	KBU 909P
7290	WWH 55L	7350	YNA 305M	7410	YNA 365M	7469	KBU 910P
7291	WWH 56L	7351	YNA 306M	7411	YNA 366M	7470	LJA 470P
7292	WWH 57L	7352	YNA 307M	7412	YNA 367M	7471	LJA 471P
7293	WWH 58L	7353	YNA 308M	7413	YNA 368M	7472	LJA 472P
7294	WWH 59L	7354	YNA 309M	7414	YNA 369M	7473	LJA 473P
7295	WWH 60L	7355	YNA 310M	7415	YNA 370M	7474	LJA 474P
7296	WWH 61L	7356	YNA 311M	7416	BNE 732N	7475	LJA 475P
7297	WWH 62L	7357	YNA 312M	7417	BNE 733N	7476	LJA 476P
7298	WWH 63L	7358	YNA 313M	7418	BNE 734N	7477	LJA 477P
7299	WWH 64L	7359	YNA 314M	7419	BNE 735N	7478	LJA 478P
7300	XJA 556L	7360	YNA 315M	7420	BNE 736N	7479	LJA 479P
7301	XJA 557L	7361	YNA 316M	7421	BNE 737N	7480	LJA 480P
7302	XJA 558L	7362	YNA 317M	7422	GNC 287N	7481	LJA 481P
7303	XJA 559L	7363	YNA 318M	7423	GNC 288N	7482	LJA 482P
7304	XJA 560L	7364	YNA 319M	7424	BNE 740N	7483	LJA 483P
7305	XJA 561L	7365	YNA 320M	7425	BNE 741N	7484	LJA 484P
7306	XJA 562L	7366	YNA 321M	7426	BNE 742N	7485	PRJ 485R
7307	XJA 563L	7367	YNA 322M	7427	GNC 289N	7486	PRJ 486R
7308	XJA 564L	7368	YNA 323M	7428	GNC 294N	7487	PRJ 487R
7309	XJA 565L	7369	YNA 324M	7429	GND 489N	7488	PRJ 488R
7310	XJA 566L	7370	YNA 325M	7430	GND 490N	7489	PRJ 489R
7311	XJA 567L	7371	YNA 326M	7431	GND 491N	7490	PRJ 490R
7312	XJA 568L	7372	YNA 327M	7432	GND 492N	7491	PRJ 491R
7313	XJA 569L	7373	YNA 328M	7433	GND 493N	7492	PRJ 492R
7314	XJA 570L	7374	YNA 329M	7434	GND 500N	7493	PRJ 493R
7315	XJA 571L	7375	YNA 330M	7435	GND 501N	7494	PRJ 494R
7316	XJA 572L	7376	YNA 331M	7436	GND 502N	7495	PRJ 495R
7317	XJA 573L	7377	YNA 332M	7437	GND 503N	7496	PRJ 496R
7318	XJA 574L	7378	YNA 333M	7438	GND 504N	7497	PRJ 497R
7319	XJA 575L	7379	YNA 334M	7439	GND 505N	7498	PRJ 498R
7320	XJA 576L	7380	YNA 335M	7440	GND 506N	7499	PRJ 499R
7321	XJA 577L	7381	YNA 336M	7441	GND 507N	7500	PRJ 500R
7322	XJA 578L	7382	YNA 337M				

7501-7559

Chassis: Leyland 'Atlantean' AN68/1R built 1974/1975
Body: Northern Counties H43/32F

7501	BNE 751N	7516	GND 497N	7531	GDB 178N	7546	HNB 36N
7502	BNE 752N	7517	GND 498N	7532	GDB 179N	7547	HNB 37N
7503	BNE 753N	7518	GND 499N	7533	GDB 180N	7548	HNB 38N
7504	BNE 754N	7519	GND 510N	7534	GDB 181N	7549	HNB 39N
7505	BNE 755N	7520	GDB 167N	7535	HNB 25N	7550	HNB 40N
7506	BNE 756N	7521	GDB 168N	7536	HNB 26N	7551	HNB 41N
7507	BNE 757N	7522	GDB 169N	7537	HNB 27N	7552	HNB 42N
7508	BNE 758N	7523	GDB 170N	7538	HNB 28N	7553	HNB 43N
7509	GNC 290N	7524	GDB 171N	7539	HNB 29N	7554	HNB 44N
7510	GNC 291N	7525	GDB 172N	7540	HNB 30N	7555	HNB 45N
7511	GNC 292N	7526	GDB 173N	7541	HNB 31N	7556	HJA 112N
7512	GNC 293N	7527	GDB 174N	7542	HNB 32N	7557	HJA 113N
7513	GND 494N	7528	GDB 175N	7543	HNB 33N	7558	HJA 114N
7514	GND 495N	7529	GDB 176N	7544	HNB 34N	7559	HJA 115N
7515	GND 496N	7530	GDB 177N	7545	HNB 35N		

7560-7960

Chassis: Leyland 'Atlantean' AN68A/1R built 1975-1979
Body: (7560-7800) Northern Counties H43/32F
(7801-7960) Park Royal H43/32F

7560	JND 984N	7595	KDB 688P	7630	LJA 630P	7665	ONF 665R
7561	JND 985N	7596	KDB 689P	7631	LJA 631P	7666	ONF 666R
7562	JND 986N	7597	LNA 250P	7632	LJA 632P	7667	ONF 667R
7563	JND 987N	7598	LNA 251P	7633	LJA 633P	7668	ONF 668R
7564	JND 988N	7599	LNA 252P	7634	LJA 634P	7669	ONF 669R
7565	JND 989N	7600	LJA 600P	7635	LJA 635P	7670	ONF 670R
7566	JND 990N	7601	LJA 601P	7636	LJA 636P	7671	ONF 671R
7567	JDB 112N	7602	LJA 602P	7637	LJA 637P	7672	ONF 672R
7568	JDB 113N	7603	LJA 603P	7638	LJA 638P	7673	ONF 673R
7569	JDB 114N	7604	LJA 604P	7639	LJA 639P	7674	ONF 674R
7570	JDB 115N	7605	LJA 605P	7640	LJA 640P	7675	ONF 675R
7571	KBU 918P	7606	LJA 606P	7641	LJA 641P	7676	ONF 676R
7572	JDB 117N	7607	LJA 607P	7642	LJA 642P	7677	ONF 677R
7573	JDB 118N	7608	LJA 608P	7643	LJA 643P	7678	ONF 678R
7574	JDB 119N	7609	LJA 609P	7644	LJA 644P	7679	ONF 679R
7575	JDB 120N	7610	LJA 610P	7645	LJA 645P	7680	ONF 680R
7576	JDB 121N	7611	LJA 611P	7646	LJA 646P	7681	ONF 681R
7577	JDB 122N	7612	LJA 612P	7647	LJA 647P	7682	ONF 682R
7578	JVM 989N	7613	LJA 613P	7648	LJA 648P	7683	ONF 683R
7579	JVM 990N	7614	LJA 614P	7649	LJA 649P	7684	ONF 684R
7580	KBU 911P	7615	LJA 615P	7650	LJA 650P	7685	ONF 685R
7581	KBU 912P	7616	LJA 616P	7651	LJA 651P	7686	ONF 686R
7582	KBU 913P	7617	LJA 617P	7652	LJA 652P	7687	ONF 687R
7583	KBU 914P	7618	LJA 618P	7653	ONF 653R	7688	ONF 688R
7584	KBU 915P	7619	LJA 619P	7654	ONF 654R	7689	ONF 689R
7585	KBU 916P	7620	LJA 620P	7655	ONF 655R	7690	ONF 690R
7586	KBU 917P	7621	LJA 621P	7656	ONF 656R	7691	ONF 691R
7587	KDB 680P	7622	LJA 622P	7657	ONF 657R	7692	ONF 692R
7588	KDB 681P	7623	LJA 623P	7658	ONF 658R	7693	ONF 693R
7589	KDB 682P	7624	LJA 624P	7659	ONF 659R	7694	ONF 694R
7590	KDB 683P	7625	LJA 625P	7660	ONF 660R	7695	ONF 695R
7591	KDB 684P	7626	LJA 626P	7661	ONF 661R	7696	ONF 696R
7592	KDB 685P	7627	LJA 627P	7662	ONF 662R	7697	ONF 697R
7593	KDB 686P	7628	LJA 628P	7663	ONF 663R	7698	ONF 698R
7594	KDB 687P	7629	LJA 629P	7664	ONF 664R	7699	ONF 699R

7700	ONF 700R	7761	UNA 761S	7822	UNA 822S	7883	WVM 883S
7701	RJA 701R	7762	UNA 762S	7823	UNA 823S	7884	WVM 884S
7702	RJA 702R	7763	UNA 763S	7824	UNA 824S	7885	WVM 885S
7703	RJA 703R	7764	UNA 764S	7825	UNA 825S	7886	WVM 886S
7704	RJA 704R	7765	UNA 765S	7826	UNA 826S	7887	WVM 887S
7705	RJA 705R	7766	UNA 766S	7827	UNA 827S	7888	WVM 888S
7706	RJA 706R	7767	UNA 767S	7828	UNA 828S	7889	WVM 889S
7707	RJA 707R	7768	UNA 768S	7829	UNA 829S	7890	WVM 890S
7708	RJA 708R	7769	UNA 769S	7830	UNA 830S	7891	WVM 891S
7709	RJA 709R	7770	UNA 770S	7831	UNA 831S	7892	WVM 892S
7710	RJA 710R	7771	UNA 771S	7832	UNA 832S	7893	WVM 893S
7711	RJA 711R	7772	UNA 772S	7833	UNA 833S	7894	WVM 894S
7712	RJA 712R	7773	UNA 773S	7834	UNA 834S	7895	WVM 895S
7713	RJA 713R	7774	UNA 774S	7835	UNA 835S	7896	WVM 896S
7714	RJA 714R	7775	UNA 775S	7836	UNA 836S	7897	WVM 897S
7715	RJA 715R	7776	UNA 776S	7837	UNA 837S	7898	WVM 898S
7716	RJA 716R	7777	UNA 777S	7838	UNA 838S	7899	WVM 899S
7717	RJA 717R	7778	UNA 778S	7839	UNA 839S	7900	WVM 900S
7718	RJA 718R	7779	UNA 779S	7840	UNA 840S	7901	WVM 901S
7719	RJA 719R	7780	UNA 780S	7841	UNA 841S	7902	WVM 902S
7720	RJA 720R	7781	UNA 781S	7842	UNA 842S	7903	ANC 903T
7721	RJA 721R	7782	UNA 782S	7843	UNA 843S	7904	ANC 904T
7722	RJA 722R	7783	UNA 783S	7844	UNA 844S	7905	ANC 905T
7723	RJA 723R	7784	UNA 784S	7845	UNA 845S	7906	ANC 906T
7724	RJA 724R	7785	UNA 785S	7846	UNA 846S	7907	ANC 907T
7725	RJA 725R	7786	UNA 786S	7847	UNA 847S	7908	ANC 908T
7726	RJA 726R	7787	UNA 787S	7848	UNA 848S	7909	ANC 909T
7727	RJA 727R	7788	UNA 788S	7849	UNA 849S	7910	ANC 910T
7728	RJA 728R	7789	UNA 789S	7850	UNA 850S	7911	ANC 911T
7729	RJA 729R	7790	UNA 790S	7851	UNA 851S	7912	ANC 912T
7730	RJA 730R	7791	UNA 791S	7852	UNA 852S	7913	ANC 913T
7731	SRJ 731R	7792	UNA 792S	7853	UNA 853S	7914	ANC 914T
7732	SRJ 732R	7793	UNA 793S	7854	UNA 854S	7915	ANC 915T
7733	SRJ 733R	7794	UNA 794S	7855	UNA 855S	7916	ANC 916T
7734	SRJ 734R	7795	UNA 795S	7856	UNA 856S	7917	ANC 917T
7735	SRJ 735R	7796	UNA 796S	7857	UNA 857S	7918	ANC 918T
7736	SRJ 736R	7797	UNA 797S	7858	UNA 858S	7919	ANC 919T
7737	SRJ 737R	7798	UNA 798S	7859	UNA 859S	7920	ANC 920T
7738	SRJ 738R	7799	UNA 799S	7860	UNA 860S	7921	ANC 921T
7739	SRJ 739R	7800	UNA 800S	7861	UNA 861S	7922	ANC 922T
7740	SRJ 740R	7801	RJA 801R	7862	UNA 862S	7923	ANC 923T
7741	SRJ 741R	7802	RJA 802R	7863	UNA 863S	7924	ANC 924T
7742	SRJ 742R	7803	RJA 803R	7864	UNA 864S	7925	ANC 925T
7743	SRJ 743R	7804	RJA 804R	7865	UNA 865S	7926	ANC 926T
7744	SRJ 744R	7805	RJA 805R	7866	UNA 866S	7927	ANC 927T
7745	SRJ 745R	7806	RJA 806R	7867	UNA 867S	7928	ANC 928T
7746	SRJ 746R	7807	RJA 807R	7868	UNA 868S	7929	ANC 929T
7747	SRJ 747R	7808	RJA 808R	7869	UNA 869S	7930	ANC 930T
7748	SRJ 748R	7809	RJA 809R	7870	UNA 870S	7931	ANC 931T
7749	SRJ 749R	7810	RJA 810R	7871	UNA 871S	7932	ANC 932T
7750	SRJ 750R	7811	RJA 811R	7872	UNA 872S	7933	BNC 933T
7751	SRJ 751R	7812	RJA 812R	7873	WVM 873S	7934	BNC 934T
7752	SRJ 752R	7813	RJA 813R	7874	WVM 874S	7935	BNC 935T
7753	SRJ 753R	7814	RJA 814R	7875	WVM 875S	7936	BNC 936T
7754	SRJ 754R	7815	RJA 815R	7876	WVM 876S	7937	BNC 937T
7755	SRJ 755R	7816	RJA 816R	7877	WVM 877S	7938	BNC 938T
7756	SRJ 756R	7817	UNA 817S	7878	WVM 878S	7939	BNC 939T
7757	SRJ 757R	7818	UNA 818S	7879	WVM 879S	7940	BNC 940T
7758	SRJ 758R	7819	UNA 819S	7880	WVM 880S	7941	BNC 941T
7759	SRJ 759R	7820	UNA 820S	7881	WVM 881S	7942	BNC 942T
7760	SRJ 760R	7821	UNA 821S	7882	WVM 882S	7943	BNC 943T

7944	BNC 944T	7949	BNC 949T	7953	BNC 953T	7957	BNC 957T
7945	BNC 945T	7950	BNC 950T	7954	BNC 954T	7958	BNC 958T
7946	BNC 946T	7951	BNC 951T	7955	BNC 955T	7959	BNC 959T
7947	BNC 947T	7952	BNC 952T	7956	BNC 956T	7960	BNC 960T
7948	BNC 948T						

8001-8020

Chassis: Daimler 'Fleetline' FE30GR built 1978
Body: Northern Counties H43/32F

8001	XBU 1S	8006	XBU 6S	8011	XBU 11S	8016	XBU 16S
8002	XBU 2S	8007	XBU 7S	8012	XBU 12S	8017	XBU 17S
8003	XBU 3S	8008	XBU 8S	8013	XBU 13S	8018	XBU 18S
8004	XBU 4S	8009	XBU 9S	8014	XBU 14S	8019	XBU 19S
8005	XBU 5S	8010	XBU 10S	8015	XBU 15S	8020	XBU 20S

8021-8150

Chassis: Leyland 'Fleetline' FE30GR built 1978-1980
Body: Northern Counties H43/32F

8021	ANA 21T	8054	BVR 54T	8087	BVR 87T	8119	HDB 119V
8022	ANA 22T	8055	BVR 55T	8088	BVR 88T	8120	HDB 120V
8023	ANA 23T	8056	BVR 56T	8089	BVR 89T	8121	HDB 121V
8024	ANA 24T	8057	BVR 57T	8090	BVR 90T	8122	HDB 122V
8025	ANA 25T	8058	BVR 58T	8091	BVR 91T	8123	HDB 123V
8026	ANA 26T	8059	BVR 59T	8092	BVR 92T	8124	HDB 124V
8027	ANA 27T	8060	BVR 60T	8093	BVR 93T	8125	HDB 125V
8028	ANA 28T	8061	BVR 61T	8094	BVR 94T	8126	HDB 126V
8029	ANA 29T	8062	BVR 62T	8095	BVR 95T	8127	KDB 127V
8030	ANA 30T	8063	BVR 63T	8096	BVR 96T	8128	KDB 128V
8031	ANA 31T	8064	BVR 64T	8097	BVR 97T	8129	KDB 129V
8032	ANA 32T	8065	BVR 65T	8098	BVR 98T	8130	KDB 130V
8033	ANA 33T	8066	BVR 66T	8099	BVR 99T	8131	KDB 131V
8034	ANA 34T	8067	BVR 67T	8100	BVR 100T	8132	KDB 132V
8035	ANA 35T	8068	BVR 68T	8101	HDB 101V	8133	KDB 133V
8036	ANA 36T	8069	BVR 69T	8102	HDB 102V	8134	KDB 134V
8037	ANA 37T	8070	BVR 70T	8103	HDB 103V	8135	KDB 135V
8038	ANA 38T	8071	BVR 71T	8104	HDB 104V	8136	KDB 136V
8039	ANA 39T	8072	BVR 72T	8105	HDB 105V	8137	KDB 137V
8040	ANA 40T	8073	BVR 73T	8106	HDB 106V	8138	KDB 138V
8041	ANA 41T	8074	BVR 74T	8107	HDB 107V	8139	KDB 139V
8042	ANA 42T	8075	BVR 75T	8108	HDB 108V	8140	KDB 140V
8043	ANA 43T	8076	BVR 76T	8109	HDB 109V	8141	GNF 16V
8044	ANA 44T	8077	BVR 77T	8110	HDB 110V	8142	GNF 17V
8045	ANA 45T	8078	BVR 78T	8111	HDB 111V	8143	MNC 486W
8046	ANA 46T	8079	BVR 79T	8112	HDB 112V	8144	MNC 487W
8047	ANA 47T	8080	BVR 80T	8113	HDB 113V	8145	MNC 488W
8048	ANA 48T	8081	BVR 81T	8114	HDB 114V	8146	MNC 489W
8049	ANA 49T	8082	BVR 82T	8115	HDB 115V	8147	MNC 490W
8050	ANA 50T	8083	BVR 83T	8116	HDB 116V	8148	MNC 491W
8051	BVR 51T	8084	BVR 84T	8117	HDB 117V	8149	MNC 492W
8052	BVR 52T	8085	BVR 85T	8118	HDB 118V	8150	MNC 493W
8053	BVR 53T	8086	BVR 86T				

8151-8525

Chassis: Leyland 'Atlantean' AN68A/1R (8425/8448/
8449/8455/8456/8460-8466/8468-8472/
8474-8478/8480/8481/8483-8485/8490/
8493/8494/8501-8525 are AN68B/1R)built
1978-1982
Body: Northern Counties H43/32F

8151	VBA 151S	8153	VBA 153S	8155	VBA 155S	8157	VBA 157S
8152	VBA 152S	8154	VBA 154S	8156	VBA 156S	8158	VBA 158S

8159	VBA 159S	8220	ANA 220T	8281	FVR 281V	8342	MNC 542W	
8160	VBA 160S	8221	ANA 221T	8282	FVR 282V	8343	MNC 543W	
8161	VBA 161S	8222	ANA 222T	8283	FVR 283V	8344	MNC 544W	
8162	VBA 162S	8223	ANA 223T	8284	FVR 284V	8345	MNC 545W	
8163	VBA 163S	8224	ANA 224T	8285	FVR 285V	8346	MNC 546W	
8164	VBA 164S	8225	ANA 225T	8286	FVR 286V	8347	MNC 547W	
8165	VBA 165S	8226	ANA 226T	8287	FVR 287V	8348	MNC 548W	
8166	VBA 166S	8227	ANA 227T	8288	FVR 288V	8349	MNC 549W	
8167	VBA 167S	8228	ANA 228T	8289	FVR 289V	8350	MNC 550W	
8168	VBA 168S	8229	ANA 229T	8290	FVR 290V	8351	ORJ 351W	
8169	VBA 169S	8230	ANA 230T	8291	FVR 291V	8352	ORJ 352W	
8170	VBA 170S	8231	ANA 231T	8292	FVR 292V	8353	ORJ 353W	
8171	VBA 171S	8232	ANA 232T	8293	FVR 293V	8354	ORJ 354W	
8172	VBA 172S	8233	ANA 233T	8294	FVR 294V	8355	ORJ 355W	
8173	VBA 173S	8234	ANA 234T	8295	FVR 295V	8356	ORJ 356W	
8174	VBA 174S	8235	ANA 235T	8296	FVR 296V	8357	ORJ 357W	
8175	VBA 175S	8236	ANA 236T	8297	FVR 297V	8358	ORJ 358W	
8176	VBA 176S	8237	ANA 237T	8298	FVR 298V	8359	ORJ 359W	
8177	VBA 177S	8238	ANA 238T	8299	FVR 299V	8360	ORJ 360W	
8178	VBA 178S	8239	ANA 239T	8300	FVR 300V	8361	ORJ 361W	
8179	VBA 179S	8240	FVR 240V	8301	KDB 301V	8362	ORJ 362W	
8180	VBA 180S	8241	ANA 241T	8302	KDB 302V	8363	ORJ 363W	
8181	VBA 181S	8242	FVR 242V	8303	KDB 303V	8364	ORJ 364W	
8182	VBA 182S	8243	FVR 243V	8304	MNC 504W	8365	ORJ 365W	
8183	VBA 183S	8244	FVR 244V	8305	MNC 505W	8366	ORJ 366W	
8184	VBA 184S	8245	FVR 245V	8306	MNC 506W	8367	ORJ 367W	
8185	VBA 185S	8246	FVR 246V	8307	MNC 507W	8368	ORJ 368W	
8186	VBA 186S	8247	FVR 247V	8308	MNC 508W	8369	ORJ 369W	
8187	VBA 187S	8248	FVR 248V	8309	MNC 509W	8370	ORJ 370W	
8188	VBA 188S	8249	FVR 249V	8310	MNC 510W	8371	ORJ 371W	
8189	VBA 189S	8250	FVR 250V	8311	MNC 511W	8372	ORJ 372W	
8190	VBA 190S	8251	FVR 251V	8312	MNC 512W	8373	ORJ 373W	
8191	VBA 191S	8252	FVR 252V	8313	MNC 513W	8374	ORJ 374W	
8192	VBA 192S	8253	FVR 253V	8314	MNC 514W	8375	ORJ 375W	
8193	VBA 193S	8254	FVR 254V	8315	MNC 515W	8376	ORJ 376W	
8194	VBA 194S	8255	FVR 255V	8316	MNC 516W	8377	ORJ 377W	
8195	VBA 195S	8256	FVR 256V	8317	MNC 517W	8378	ORJ 378W	
8196	VBA 196S	8257	FVR 257V	8318	MNC 518W	8379	ORJ 379W	
8197	VBA 197S	8258	FVR 258V	8319	MNC 519W	8380	ORJ 380W	
8198	VBA 198S	8259	FVR 259V	8320	MNC 520W	8381	ORJ 381W	
8199	VBA 199S	8260	FVR 260V	8321	MNC 521W	8382	ORJ 382W	
8200	VBA 200S	8261	FVR 261V	8322	MNC 522W	8383	ORJ 383W	
8201	XRJ 201S	8262	FVR 262V	8323	MNC 523W	8384	ORJ 384W	
8202	XRJ 202S	8263	FVR 263V	8324	MNC 524W	8385	ORJ 385W	
8203	XRJ 203S	8264	FVR 264V	8325	MNC 525W	8386	ORJ 386W	
8204	XRJ 204S	8265	FVR 265V	8326	MNC 526W	8387	ORJ 387W	
8205	XRJ 205S	8266	FVR 266V	8327	MNC 527W	8388	ORJ 388W	
8206	XRJ 206S	8267	FVR 267V	8328	MNC 528W	8389	ORJ 389W	
8207	ANA 207T	8268	FVR 268V	8329	MNC 529W	8390	ORJ 390W	
8208	ANA 208T	8269	FVR 269V	8330	MNC 530W	8391	ORJ 391W	
8209	ANA 209T	8270	FVR 270V	8331	MNC 531W	8392	ORJ 392W	
8210	ANA 210T	8271	FVR 271V	8332	MNC 532W	8393	ORJ 393W	
8211	ANA 211T	8272	FVR 272V	8333	MNC 533W	8394	ORJ 394W	
8212	ANA 212T	8273	FVR 273V	8334	MNC 534W	8395	ORJ 395W	
8213	ANA 213T	8274	FVR 274V	8335	MNC 535W	8396	ORJ 396W	
8214	ANA 214T	8275	FVR 275V	8336	MNC 536W	8397	ORJ 397W	
8215	ANA 215T	8276	FVR 276V	8337	MNC 537W	8398	ORJ 398W	
8216	ANA 216T	8277	FVR 277V	8338	MNC 538W	8399	ORJ 399W	
8217	ANA 217T	8278	FVR 278V	8339	MNC 539W	8400	ORJ 400W	
8218	ANA 218T	8279	FVR 279V	8340	MNC 540W	8401	MRJ 401W	
8219	ANA 219T	8280	FVR 280V	8341	MNC 541W	8402	MRJ 402W	

8403	MRJ 403W	8434	SND 434X	8465	SND 465X	8496	SND 496X
8404	MRJ 404W	8435	SND 435X	8466	SND 466X	8497	SND 497X
8405	MRJ 405W	8436	SND 436X	8467	SND 467X	8498	SND 498X
8406	MRJ 406W	8437	SND 437X	8468	SND 468X	8499	SND 499X
8407	MRJ 407W	8438	SND 438X	8469	SND 469X	8500	SND 500X
8408	MRJ 408W	8439	SND 439X	8470	SND 470X	8501	SND 501X
8409	MRJ 409W	8440	SND 440X	8471	SND 471X	8502	SND 502X
8410	MRJ 410W	8441	SND 441X	8472	SND 472X	8503	SND 503X
8411	MRJ 411W	8442	SND 442X	8473	SND 473X	8504	SND 504X
8412	SND 412X	8443	SND 443X	8474	SND 474X	8505	SND 505X
8413	SND 413X	8444	SND 444X	8475	SND 475X	8506	SND 506X
8414	SND 414X	8445	SND 445X	8476	SND 476X	8507	SND 507X
8415	SND 415X	8446	SND 446X	8477	SND 477X	8508	SND 508X
8416	SND 416X	8447	SND 447X	8478	SND 478X	8509	SND 509X
8417	SND 417X	8448	SND 448X	8479	SND 479X	8510	SND 510X
8418	SND 418X	8449	SND 449X	8480	SND 480X	8511	SND 511X
8419	SND 419X	8450	SND 450X	8481	SND 481X	8512	SND 512X
8420	SND 420X	8451	SND 451X	8482	SND 482X	8513	SND 513X
8421	SND 421X	8452	SND 452X	8483	SND 483X	8514	SND 514X
8422	SND 422X	8453	SND 453X	8484	SND 484X	8515	SND 515X
8423	SND 423X	8454	SND 454X	8485	SND 485X	8516	SND 516X
8424	SND 424X	8455	SND 455X	8486	SND 486X	8517	SND 517X
8425	SND 425X	8456	SND 456X	8487	SND 487X	8518	SND 518X
8426	SND 426X	8457	SND 457X	8488	SND 488X	8519	SND 519X
8427	SND 427X	8458	SND 458X	8489	SND 489X	8520	SND 520X
8428	SND 428X	8459	SND 459X	8490	SND 490X	8521	SND 521X
8429	SND 429X	8460	SND 460X	8491	SND 491X	8522	SND 522X
8430	SND 430X	8461	SND 461X	8492	SND 492X	8523	SND 523X
8431	SND 431X	8462	SND 462X	8493	SND 493X	8524	SND 524X
8432	SND 432X	8463	SND 463X	8494	SND 494X	8525	SND 525X
8433	SND 433X	8464	SND 464X	8495	SND 495X		

8526-8825

Chassis: Leyland 'Atlantean' AN68D/1R built 1982 and on order
Body: Northern Counties H43/32F

8526	SND 526X	8550	ANA 550Y	8574	ANA 574Y	8598	ANA 598Y
8527	SND 527X	8551	ANA 551Y	8575	ANA 575Y	8599	ANA 599Y
8528	SND 528X	8552	ANA 552Y	8576	ANA 576Y	8600	ANA 600Y
8529	SND 529X	8553	ANA 553Y	8577	ANA 577Y	8601	ANA 601Y
8530	SND 530X	8554	ANA 554Y	8578	ANA 578Y	8602	ANA 602Y
8531	ANA 531Y	8555	ANA 555Y	8579	ANA 579Y	8603	ANA 603Y
8532	ANA 532Y	8556	ANA 556Y	8580	ANA 580Y	8604	ANA 604Y
8533	ANA 533Y	8557	ANA 557Y	8581	ANA 581Y	8605	ANA 605Y
8534	ANA 534Y	8558	ANA 558Y	8582	ANA 582Y	8606	ANA 606Y
8535	ANA 535Y	8559	ANA 559Y	8583	ANA 583Y	8607	ANA 607Y
8536	ANA 536Y	8560	ANA 560Y	8584	ANA 584Y	8608	ANA 608Y
8537	ANA 537Y	8561	ANA 561Y	8585	ANA 585Y	8609	ANA 609Y
8538	ANA 538Y	8562	ANA 562Y	8586	ANA 586Y	8610	ANA 610Y
8539	ANA 539Y	8563	ANA 563Y	8587	ANA 587Y	8611	ANA 611Y
8540	ANA 540Y	8564	ANA 564Y	8588	ANA 588Y	8612	ANA 612Y
8541	ANA 541Y	8565	ANA 565Y	8589	ANA 589Y	8613	ANA 613Y
8542	ANA 542Y	8566	ANA 566Y	8590	ANA 590Y	8614	ANA 614Y
8543	ANA 543Y	8567	ANA 567Y	8591	ANA 591Y	8615	ANA 615Y
8544	ANA 544Y	8568	ANA 568Y	8592	ANA 592Y	8616	ANA 616Y
8545	ANA 545Y	8569	ANA 569Y	8593	ANA 593Y	8617	ANA 617Y
8546	ANA 546Y	8570	ANA 570Y	8594	ANA 594Y	8618	ANA 618Y
8547	ANA 547Y	8571	ANA 571Y	8595	ANA 595Y	8619	ANA 619Y
8548	ANA 548Y	8572	ANA 572Y	8596	ANA 596Y	8620	ANA 620Y
8549	ANA 549Y	8573	ANA 573Y	8597	ANA 597Y	8621	ANA 621Y

8622 ANA 622Y	8673	8724	8775
8623 ANA 623Y	8674	8725	8776
8624 ANA 624Y	8675	8726	8777
8625 ANA 625Y	8676	8727	8778
8626 ANA 626Y	8677	8728	8779
8627 ANA 627Y	8678	8729	8780
8628 ANA 628Y	8679	8730	8781
8629 ANA 629Y	8680	8731	8782
8630 ANA 630Y	8681	8732	8783
8631	8682	8733	8784
8632	8683	8734	8785
8633	8684	8735	8786
8634	8685	8736	8787
8635	8686	8737	8788
8636	8687	8738	8789
8637	8688	8739	8790
8638	8689	8740	8791
8639	8690	8741	8792
8640	8691	8742	8793
8641	8692	8743	8794
8642	8693	8744	8795
8643	8694	8745	8796
8644	8695	8746	8797
8645	8696	8747	8798
8646	8697	8748	8799
8647	8698	8749	8800
8648	8699	8750	8801
8649	8700	8751	8802
8650	8701	8752	8803
8651	8702	8753	8804
8652	8703	8754	8805
8653	8704	8755	8806
8654	8705	8756	8807
8655	8706	8757	8808
8656	8707	8758	8809
8657	8708	8759	8810
8658	8709	8760	8811
8659	8710	8761	8812
8660	8711	8762	8813
8661	8712	8763	8814
8662	8713	8764	8815
8663	8714	8765	8816
8664	8715	8766	8817
8665	8716	8767	8818
8666	8717	8768	8819
8667	8718	8769	8820
8668	8719	8770	8821
8669	8720	8771	8822
8670	8721	8772	8823
8671	8722	8773	8824
8672	8723	8774	8825

A Mayne & Son Ltd

Mayne's was established in 1920 as a road haulage business, and shortly afterwards began carrying passengers, in lorries with demountable bus bodies. In 1925 'proper' passenger vehicles arrived, and by the following year the company was operating a regular stage service between Manchester city centre and Audenshaw (Kershaw Lane) via Ashton New Road. There were several other independent stage operators in the Manchester area at that time, but all except Mayne's had been purchased by the various municipal transport undertakings by 1944.

The headquarters was in the Bradford area of the city, the garage being situated in Queen Street just off Ashton New Road until the present premises near Edge Lane were acquired in 1938. The company developed a shuttle service between Edge Lane and Droylsden; this was extended inwards from Edge Lane to Manchester (Stevenson Square) on 27th January 1958, and was jointly operated by Mayne's and Manchester City Transport as service 46 for the next eight years.

For many years the Ashton New Road services have been operated by double-deckers and AECs were the favoured make until recently. However, the last few AEC 'Regents, fitted with handsome rear-entrance East Lancs bodies, have been withdrawn in the last few years; the last two to be owned, 8859/8860 VR, have gone for preservation, although 8859 is still owned by Mayne's. Coincidentally the last single-deck AEC, 'Reliance' FBU 304K of 1972, has also been withdrawn since our last edition. The double-deck fleet now consists of five Daimler 'Fleetlines' with Roe bodies, and five Bristol VRs with ECW semi-coach bodies. The single-deck coach fleet included some early Dennises and Talbots, but since the Second World War Bedfords have been predominant, with contributions from AEC, Bristol and most recently Leyland.

The Stevenson Square - Droylsden service is still jointly operated with Greater Manchester Transport as successors to MCT, but since 1966 Mayne's have operated all the mileage on it. In that year, when MCT's trolleybuses were withdrawn from the Ashton New Road services, the Corporation surrendered its workings on the joint service in return for the takeover of Mayne's older service to Kershaw Lane. This was numbered 214 and extended a few hundred yards to the Ryecroft Hall terminus, but since 1966 it has operated at Monday to Friday peak periods only. At the same time the joint service 46 was renumbered 213.

An extension of Mayne's service network took place in 1979 when a new service 209 was introduced between Manchester (Stevenson Square) and Lumb Mill, on the Droylsden - Littlemoss - Ashton road. This service was established with the acquiescence of the PTE; like the 213 it operates jointly with the PTE and the PTE's special tickets and passes are accepted, but Mayne's operate all the mileage. About a year later the 209's outer terminus was extended to Hartshead, north of Ashton-under-Lyne, providing a direct link to Manchester from this area for the first time. Starting a new service with PTE support must be an unusual activity for an independent bus company in a metropolitan area. The service operates every day (except Sundays and bank holidays) on a frequency varying from 30 mins. in peak hours to 45 mins. on Saturdays and approximately 60 mins. at off-peak times on Mondays to Fridays; the regular service stops in the early evening and there is only one late-night trip in each direction.

ese next three views
m to show how much
riety there really
 in the PTE's so-
lled 'standard' class-
. Some early 'stand-
ds' like 7222 (VNB
3L) were fitted with
ntre exits, thought
 be essential for
sy routes in Manches-
r and Salford. Evid-
tly they are less
cessary than was once
ought! 7222 is in
rtland Street, Manche-
er. (A M WITTON)

out 1977 the rate
 delivery of Northern
unties bodies slowed
own, and an order was
aced for 160 Park
yal-bodied Atlanteans
 go with the 200 Park
yal bodies ordered
 the outset. Although
tandard parts are used
erever possible, the
odies are easily dist-
nguishable. 7929 (ANC
29T), with monster
umber transfers on
ts front and rear domes
 aid identification,
nters Stockport bus
tation. (A M WITTON)

ince about fleet number
430, new 'Standards'
ave arrived from North-
rn Counties with bodies
uilt of light alloy
o a different design.
he two-piece windows
t the front of the
pper deck are the most
bvious feature identi-
ying these buses. 8477
SND 477X) arrives in
iccadilly Gardens bus
tation, Manchester,
ith a 'Mancunian' be-
ind. (A M WITTON)

Mayne's of Manchester have had many different makes of bus in their long and illustrious history, but this is probably their first Mercedes! It is a mini bus which brings an end a succession of Ford 'Transits' owned one at a time, and used for small party private hire. LDJ 723W is posed outside the garage in Ashton New Road, Clayton. (D AKRIGG)

The visit of Pope John Paul II to Heaton Park in 1982 made history in many ways. Apart from the obvious religious significance, it afforded an opportunity to transport enthusiasts to walk along the fast lanes of two local motorways without getting mown down! National Travel (West) N225 (WUE 612S) was parked on the A627M near Slattocks for the Papal Visit. It is a Leopard PSU5 with Willowbrook body. (A M WITTON)

The PSU5 remains the standard coach for National Travel (West), although Tigers and Dennis Falcons are now arriving. 'Leopard' N287 (SND 287X), since renumbered like the one above, poses outside Chorlton Street coach station. It carries Duple 'Dominant' coachwork. (A M WITTON)

The two large coach companies featured in this book for the first time have such extensive touring commitments that it is almost more likely to find their coaches outside Greater Manchester than inside it! Shearings 321 (JDB 937V), a Plaxton-bodied Ford and therefore typical of the majority of the fleet, poses in Newbury with tour passengers for the Isle of Wight. (D AKRIGG)

Like many other former AEC Reliance users, Smith's of Wigan has switched to Volvo for each of their present vehicle intake. 209 (TND 123X), a Volvo B58 with Duple body, is parked in Vauxhall Bridge coach park, London, while its passengers sampled the delights of the capital city on a 5-day tour. A large order for Volvo coaches has been made for 1983 delivery. (A M WITTON)

Only two of Yelloway's present fleet carry Duple bodies. One of them, NNC 850P, an AEC Reliance like most of the fleet, is seen in the back-streets of Rochdale near the Weir Street premises which are the nerve centre of this well-known firm. (D AKRIGG)

Bury's green buses were mostly Weymann-bodied Leylands in the post-war period, until East Lancs bodywork became predominant from 1965 on. 158 (EN 9958), a Leyland PD2/4 built in 1949, waits in Kay Gardens, Bury. Before the bus station, loading points in Bury town centre surrounded all three sides of Kay Gardens and spilled into neighbouring streets. (A M WITTON)

SHMD, North Western and LUT all favoured the Atkinson single decker while it was available. This one, North Western's 361 (EDB 321), combined underfloor-engined layout with rear-entrance bodywork - a Northern peculiarity adopted by a number of undertakings in Lancashire and Yorkshire. It carried Weymann bodywork similar to the design of the Leyland 'Olympic', and was in Charles Street depot yard. (A M WITTON)

Trolleybus wires were visible until 1966 in the eastern corner of Manchester's Piccadilly Gardens, and both red and blue trolleybuses could be seen thereon. The blue ones belonged to Ashton Corporation, whose Bond-bodied BUTs like 84 (YTE 823) survived until the final closure and were marginally the newest trolleybuses in Lancashire. (A M WITTON)

Stage carriage operations nowadays account for only a minority of the Company's work; for many years Mayne's have been the principal coach operator in the East Manchester area. Many coach firms have been taken over, the most recent being Connolly's in 1971, and E Morby & Sons of Droylsden in 1974. For a couple of years the Morby company was retained, with one vehicle licensed to it, but Morby's has now ceased trading. Mayne's is now associated with Barry Cooper Coaches of Warrington, with a common board of directors. Cooper's have become famous for rebuilding and rebodying older underfloor-engined coaches, and one such vehicle has been produced by Mayne's from parts of older Leyland 'Leopards'.

Traditionally the 'stage' fleet, mainly consisting of double-deckers, was liveried in a maroon and green livery reminiscent of the old-style City of Oxford colour scheme, and one 'Fleetline' in these colours was decorated with a celebratory message in 1980, on the occasion of Mayne's 60th anniversary. However, all vehicles are now liveried in the red and cream which has long been standard for the coach fleet. The dual-purpose Bristol VRs were delivered in red and cream and were the first double-deckers to bear this livery in the Mayne's fleet. The garage and head office is at Ashton New Road, Manchester. Please note that to avoid any possible misunderstanding, Mayne's management has asked us to point out that <u>they can only accommodate enthusiast visits to the depot if arrangements are made in advance</u>. Enthusiasts asking for permission to visit without making prior bookings will, regretfully, have to be turned away.

Regn. Number	Chassis Make and Type	Body Make and Seats	Date New	Notes
LRJ 210P	Daimler 'Fleetline' CRG6LXB	Roe H44/34F	1976	
LRJ 211P	"	"	"	
LRJ 212P	"	"	"	
LRJ 213P	"	"	"	
LRJ 214P	"	"	"	
PTO 350R	Leyland 'Leopard' PSU5A/4R	Plaxton C53F	"	(a)
VJA 663S	Bedford SB5	Plaxton C41F	1978	
VJA 665S	Bristol VRTSL6LXB	ECW CH41/29F	"	
VJA 666S	"	"	"	
VJA 667S	"	"	"	
YNF 350T	Bedford SB5	Duple C41F	"	
YNF 351T	"	"	"	
HDB 354V	Leyland 'Leopard' PSU3F/5R	Plaxton C53F	1980	
HDB 355V	"	"	"	
HDB 356V	Leyland 'Leopard' PSU5C/4R	Plaxton C57F	"	
HDB 357V	"	"	"	
LDJ 723W	Mercedes-Benz	Devon 12-seat	"	(b)
MRJ 8W	Bristol VRTSL6LXB	ECW CH41/29F	"	
MRJ 9W	"	"	"	
MRJ 358W	Leyland 'Leopard' PSU3F/4R	Plaxton C53F	"	
MRJ 359W	Leyland 'Leopard' PSU5C/4R	Plaxton C57F	1981	
MRJ 360W	"	"	"	
SNC 361X	"	"	"	
SNC 362X	"	"	"	
SNC 363X	"	"	"	
SNC 364X	"	"	"	
SNC 365X	"	"	1982	
SNC 366X	Leyland 'Leopard' PSU3A/4R	Plaxton C53F	"	(c)
SND 352X	Leyland 'Tiger' TRCTL11/3R	"	"	
SND 353X	"	"	"	

NOTES:-
(a) PTO 350R was ex Kettlewell, Retford, in 1982
(b) LDJ 723W was ex O'Brien, Farnworth, in 1981
(c) SNC 366X was assembled by Mayne's from parts including some from previous vehicles, and was fitted with a new Plaxton body

National Travel (West) Ltd — Northern Unit

National Travel (West) Ltd came into being in 1977 to rationalise the NBC's regional subsidiaries, National Travel (North West) Ltd and National Travel (Midlands) Ltd. The company took over the Manchester headquarters of the former North West company, originally at Canada House, Chepstow Street, and subsequently moving to offices at Chorlton Street coach station. Since the formation of the present company, all direct coach operations in the Midlands have been given up, but it is appropriate to deal with the various companies which were taken into the two undertakings which merged to form National Travel (West).

W C Standerwick Ltd of Blackpool was founded in 1908; in 1932 it was taken over by Ribble Motor Services, by which time Standerwick's had already developed a London express service and a large fleet. Ribble kept Standerwick as a separate company, and although the subsidiary began to buy Leyland coaches instead of AECs, they continued to register them in Blackpool, not Preston. One of Standerwick's main claims to fame was through their pioneering work, from 1959 on, in developing long-distance double-deck coach operation. The first batch of these was developed out of a prototype delivered to Ribble in 1959. One of the first production Leyland 'Atlanteans', it carried a 50-seat body equipped with a toilet and refreshment servery. A batch of these vehicles followed in 1960 and took up duties on the London - Lancashire services. They were replaced in 1970-1972 by 30 Bristol VRL coaches with ECW 60-seat bodies equipped as the Atlanteans; they were noteworthy as the only production VRL models built for British undertakings, and as the only 36-foot long double-deckers. However, they were not as great a success as had been hoped, and all have been withdrawn for several years now. It is worth noting though that the Southern unit of National Travel (West), based on the remains of the Cheltenham-based South West company, has during 1982 taken delivery of a Leyland 'Olympian' with 65-seat ECW coach body. It will be interesting to see whether this type of vehicle returns in due course to North-West England and to the services on which the Atlanteans and VRLs ran for many years!

The early history of the North Western Road Car Co and its antecedents, dating back to 1913, has been recounted earlier in this book under the Greater Manchester Transport heading; SELNEC inherited most of North Western's local bus routes on the dissolution of the company in 1972. The express coaches, which served North Western's routes from Manchester to London and other long-distance runs, were retained under the North Western name. The coach company was run from headquarters which went briefly to Wilmslow and then to Preston. In October 1973 both Standerwick and North Western were separated from Ribble to form, in January 1974, National Travel (North West) Ltd., a direct subsidiary of the National Bus Company, with headquarters in Manchester.

Although the Midlands branch of the company has now ceased to exist, some account of its history is in order. National Travel (Midlands) Ltd was established in December 1973, being in fact a re-naming of South Midland Motor Services Ltd., which had been trading since 1922, was nationalised in 1950 as part of the Red & White group, and passed in 1970 into the control of City of Oxford Motor Services Ltd. Thereafter the South Midland company remained dormant (although the South Midland name is still part of the City of Oxford fleetname) until it was reactivated as National Travel (Midlands) Ltd in 1973. The Midlands company was based at Digbeth coach station in Birmingham, and was responsible for marketing, planning, booking and control of express services and tours provided by the NBC in the Midlands area. Vehicles for these services were supplied by the NBC's other subsidiaries in the Midlands area.

Early in 1974 National Travel (Midlands) acquired some vehicles of its own with the takeover of the fleet and coaching business of Everall's of Wolverhampton, and the assets of Worthington Motor Tours of Birmingham. Everall's had been started as a taxi business by the brothers Don and Cliff Everall; in 1926 they pioneered motor coach operation from Wolverhampton, and this activity grew rapidly with numerous takeovers. However, ancillary interests included travel agencies, holiday camps and a Ford main dealership; these activities are still continued privately under the Everall name.

The other acquisition, Worthington Motor Tours, stemmed from a business founded by Mr H J Lingwood in the early 1920s; in 1928 Mr J W Worthington joined him in partnership, and later in the same year Mr Worthington took over completely. The company specialised in extended tours, with a fleet mainly of Maudslay coaches and a head office at Station Garage, Stafford. The war put a temporary stop to the touring business, but in compensation Worthington's did much work for Government establishments in Staffordshire - including, it is said, 'tours' to the 'holiday camps' thoughtfully provided in the area for German prisoners of war! Worthington's headquarters moved to Wolverhampton and later to Birmingham in the post-war years, as the company took over large coaching businesses in each of these towns. Bedfords, Commers and Fords successively passed through the fleet; the Fords, some of which survived into National Travel ownership, harmonised nicely with the Everall fleet which was almost exclusively of this make. Mr Worthington died in 1971, thus hastening the sale of his creation to the National Bus Company. The new Midlands company acquired depots at Bilston (Everall's) and Hurst Street, Birmingham (Worthington's).

In 1977, as shown above, National Travel (Midlands) ceased to exist as a separate company, becoming part of National Travel (West) Ltd. In 1979 National Travel (West) gave up its direct coach operations in the Midlands area; this involved closing the Birmingham and Bilston depots, transferring some vehicles to Midland Red, bringing others to the North-West, while others again were offered for sale. The lightweight coach which formed the greater part of the Midlands fleet has now been completely eliminated by National Travel (West).

In early 1980 the company took over the Liverpool - London and other express services operated by Crosville, together with an operating base at Liverpool (Skelhorne Street) and several vehicles. A major reorganisation of the Cheltenham-based National Travel (South West) Ltd company, brought the remains of its activities into National Travel (West) Ltd, after outlying operations had been transferred to other NBC subsidiaries in South Wales and the West Country. However, the remaining bases at Cheltenham and Bristol still have a measure of local autonomy, and for the time being control of their operations is vested in the Midland Red (Express) company. The Cheltenham and Bristol units will therefore continue to be dealt with separately, in Fleetbook 12, rather than being combined with the Manchester-based fleet in this book. All vehicles of the Northern bases of National Travel (West) were given fleet numbers with an 'N' prefix, the prefix 'S' being given to vehicles of the Southern area. A further renumbering is coming into force in December 1982, and the new numbers for the Northern unit coaches are shown in the following fleet list.

The Northern units garage vehicles at Hulme Hall Road, Manchester, with outstations at the Ribble garages at Burnley and Blackpool; and at Skelhorne Street, Liverpool, with outstations at the Crosville garages at Caernarfon, Holyhead and Llandudno Junction. The fleetname is 'NATIONAL TRAVEL˙WEST', in conjunction with the white coach livery and 'NATIONAL EXPRESS' or 'NATIONAL HOLIDAYS' names towards the rear of vehicle sides. Apart from various special liveries to advertise particular National Travel services, several coaches are fitted with serveries, video screens and a special livery for use on the Rapide service between Manchester and London.

1-18

Chassis: Leyland 'Leopard' PSU5A/4R built 1976
Body: (1-5) Plaxton C51F
(6/7) Plaxton C48FT
(8-18) Duple C51F

1	SFV 201P	6	SFV 206P	11	URN 211R	15	URN 215R
2	SFV 202P	7	SFV 207P	12	URN 212R	16	URN 216R
3	SFV 203P	8	URN 208R	13	URN 213R	17	URN 217R
4	SFV 204P	9	URN 209R	14	URN 214R	18	URN 218R
5	SFV 205P	10	URN 210R				

19-23

Chassis: Leyland 'Leopard' PSU5B/4R built 1977
Body: Willowbrook C51F

| 19 | XCK 219R | 21 | XCK 221R | 22 | SEA 311R | 23 | SEA 312R |
| 20 | XCK 220R | | | | | | |

24-80

Chassis: Leyland 'Leopard' PSU5C/4R built 1977-1980
Body: (24-26) Willowbrook C51F
(27/28) Duple C46FT
(29-33) Duple C51F
(34-48) Duple C50F
(49-64) Duple C53F
(65-80) Plaxton C50F

24	WUE 611S	39	BNB 239T	53	HNE 253V	67	MRJ 267W
25	WUE 612S	40	BNB 240T	54	HNE 254V	68	MRJ 268W
26	WUE 613S	41	BNB 241T	55	HNE 255V	69	MRJ 269W
27	VVU 227S	42	BNB 242T	56	JND 256V	70	MRJ 270W
28	VVU 228S	43	BNB 243T	57	JND 257V	71	MRJ 271W
29	VVU 229S	44	BNB 244T	58	JND 258V	72	MRJ 272W
30	VVU 230S	45	BNB 245T	59	JND 259V	73	MRJ 273W
31	VVU 231S	46	BNB 246T	60	JND 260V	74	MRJ 274W
32	VVU 232S	47	BNB 247T	61	JND 261V	75	MRJ 275W
33	VVU 233S	48	BNB 248T	62	JND 262V	76	MRJ 276W
34	BNB 234T	49	HNE 249V	63	JND 263V	77	MRJ 277W
35	BNB 235T	50	HNE 250V	64	JND 264V	78	MRJ 278W
36	BNB 236T	51	HNE 251V	65	MRJ 265W	79	MRJ 279W
37	BNB 237T	52	HNE 252V	66	MRJ 266W	80	MRJ 280W
38	BNB 238T						

81-94

Chassis: Leyland 'Leopard' PSU5E/4R built 1981 and on order 1982
Body: (81-83) Duple C46FT
(84-90) Duple C50F
(91-94) ECW C53F

81	SND 281X	85	SND 285X	89	SND 289X	92	ANA 92Y
82	SND 282X	86	SND 286X	90	SND 290X	93	ANA 93Y
83	SND 283X	87	SND 287X	91	ANA 91Y	94	ANA 94Y
84	SND 284X	88	SND 288X				

95

Chassis: Leyland 'Tiger' TRCTL11/3R built 1982
Body: Duple C53F

95 WVR 60X

99-100

Chassis: Dennis 'Falcon' 5HSC built 1982
Body: Duple C47FT

99 ANA 99Y   100 ANA 100Y

117-142

Chassis: Leyland 'Leopard' PSU3B/4R built 1974
Body: Duple C49F

117	TTF 217M	128	TTF 228M	133	TTF 233M	138	TTF 238M
120	TTF 220M	129	TTF 229M	134	TTF 234M	139	TTF 239M
122	TTF 222M	130	TTF 230M	135	TTF 235M	140	TTF 240M
124	TTF 224M	131	TTF 231M	136	TTF 236M	141	UTF 721M
126	TTF 226M	132	TTF 232M	137	TTF 237M	142	UTF 722M
127	TTF 227M						

145-149

Chassis: Leyland 'Leopard' PSU3C/4R built 1976
Body: Duple C47F

145	PCK 145P	147	PCK 147P	148	PCK 148P	149	PCK 149P
146	PCK 146P						

150-160

Chassis: Leyland 'Leopard' PSU3D/4R built 1977
Body: Willowbrook C47F (159/160 are C42FT)

150	XCW 150R	153	XCW 153R	156	XCW 156R	159	VDH 243S
151	XCW 151R	154	XCW 154R	157	XCW 157R	160	VDH 244S
152	XCW 152R	155	XCW 155R	158	PWD 841R		

161-165

Chassis: Leyland 'Leopard' PSU3E/4R built 1977
Body: Duple C49F
Ex Crosville Nos. CLL321-325 in 1980

161	YTU 321S	163	YTU 323S	164	YTU 324S	165	YTU 325S
162	YTU 322S						

172-176

Chassis: Leyland 'Leopard' PSU3C/4R built 1976
Body: Duple C49F
Ex Ribble Nos. 1072-1076 in 1980

172	PCW 672P	174	PCW 674P	175	PCW 675P	176	PCW 676P
173	PCW 673P						

178-192

Chassis: Leyland 'Leopard' PSU3B/4R built 1973
Body: Duple C49F
191/192 were ex Ribble Nos. 1025/1026 in 1980
These vehicles are due for early withdrawal

178	XTF 818L	183	XTF 823L	187	XTF 827L	191	WTF 571L
182	XTF 822L	184	XTF 824L	188	XTF 828L	192	WTF 572L

Shearings Holidays Ltd

The present Shearings Holidays group traces its ancestry to a coal haulage business founded by Mr Tom Jackson, probably just after the First World War, in Moss Lane, Altrincham. In the 1920s the firm entered the passenger carrying trade, using charabanc bodies bolted on to the underframes of the coal lorries, which could thus still be used for their original purpose on weekdays. Evidently the coaching side was found profitable, and the firm began to buy coaches secondhand, although it was 1951 before the first new coach was purchased - a Leyland 'Royal Tiger' with Harrington 'dorsal fin' coachwork, not only the first new coach but probably the last Leyland of any kind to be bought new for many years.

As the business grew with the post-war coaching boom, the fleet was built up by large-scale purchases of Bedfords, which were supplanted from about 1970 onwards by Fords. The growth of Jackson's was helped along by several strategic purchases of other established coach businesses in various parts of Greater Manchester. Shearing's of Salford was acquired in 1961, and their white livery inspired part of the present colour scheme. Shearing's also contributed the first Continental tours licences to the group, laying the foundations of what is now an important part of the business. The next acquisition was Pleasureways of Oldham in 1966; their livery was yellow, once again being reflected in the present colour scheme. Finally several more Continental licences and some vehicles to work them were acquired from Ribblesdale of Blackburn in 1970; Ribblesdale however remains as a separate undertaking in Blackburn, although the Ribblesdale name is used on some Shearing's group coaches. For some years it was the practice to license a proportion of the Group fleet to each of the constituent companies - Jackson's, Shearing's, Pleasureways and Ribblesdale - although all four companies operated from the coach station in Moss Lane, Altrincham, and used the same livery and fleet numbering scheme. However, from the arrival of the 1981 delivery of new coaches, all vehicles carried Shearing's Holidays as a fleetname and were licensed to the parent company.

On 1st October 1979 Shearing's took over Ellerman Salopia Ltd, formerly a subsidiary of the Middlesbrough-based Ellerman group, with an operating base in Whitchurch, Shropshire, and a network of rural stage services which are still operated. The company name was quickly changed back to the original Salopia Saloon Coaches Ltd., which the firm had had before takeover by Ellerman's. In this case, as Whitchurch is in a different Traffic Area, Salopia coaches are licensed separately from the main fleet and the company has its own management and staff at Whitchurch; its vehicles and history are given in Fleetbook 6 - Buses of the West Midlands. Vehicles apparently 'missing' from recent series in the main Shearing's fleet are those which are allocated to Salopia at Whitchurch.

On 6th October 1980 Shearing's entered the British Coachways consortium, running services from Liverpool and Manchester to the Midlands, London and Scotland, jointly with other consortium members. Three Leyland 'Leopards' were included in the 1981 coach deliveries, mainly intended for express service work for which duties the Fords were proving unequal. More recently a large batch of DAF coaches, together with one Volvo, have accounted for the 1982 deliveries, replacing Fords for new deliveries for the first time in a dozen years. However, the British Coachways operations were discontinued in August 1982. The only regular service now operated by Shearing's is a twice daily run from Manchester Airport to Liverpool. Manchester Airport is also the scene of much crew-bus operation, mainly by Shearing's, taking airline crews from their incoming planes to hotels etc. and back again for their next flight. A fleet of minibuses of various types is kept for these duties. Especially when planes are diverted due to bad weather, Shearing's takes the lion's share of contracts for taking crews and passengers by coach to other British airports.

Shearing's is still very much a family firm despite its size; the present Managing Director, Mr Don Jackson, is the founder's son. The livery is white and yellow with marigold lining-out, and this livery also applies to the Salopia fleet. Shearing's main fleet is based at spacious premises known as The Coach Station, Moss Lane, Altrincham.

113-116

Chassis: Bedford CFL built 1978 (114), 1979 (113) and 1981 (115/116)
Body: Plaxton C17F
115/116 do not carry their fleet numbers
114 was ex Plaxton demonstration vehicle in 1981

113	FVM 191V	114	NVY 219T	115	RNE 692W	116	RNE 693W

Chassis: Bedford VAS5 built 1981
Body: Duple C29F
No fleet number is allocated

PRO 442W

Chassis: Mercedes-Benz 508D built 1982
Body: Reeves Burgess C19F
No fleet numbers are allocated

WBU 11X   ANA 112Y

318-347

Chassis: Ford R1114 built 1979/1980
Body: Plaxton C53F
347 was built on a left-hand-drive chassis rebuilt to right-hand drive by Shearing's

318	JDB 940V	322	JDB 935V	326	JDB 932V	340	JDB 946V
319	JDB 938V	323	JDB 939V	329	JDB 933V	341	JDB 947V
321	JDB 937V	325	JDB 936V	339	JDB 934V	347	DNA 482T

349

Chassis: Ford R1014 built 1979
Body: Plaxton C45F

349   EVM 442T

350-388

Chassis: Ford R1114 built 1980/1981
Body: Plaxton C53F

350	JDB 948V	365	PNB 781W	370	PNB 786W	375	PNB 791W
355	JDB 941V	366	PNB 782W	371	PNB 787W	376	PNB 792W
356	JDB 942V	367	PNB 783W	372	PNB 788W	377	PNB 793W
357	JDB 943V	368	PNB 784W	373	PNB 789W	388	PNB 804W
358	JDB 951V	369	PNB 785W	374	PNB 790W		

389-391

Chassis: Leyland 'Leopard' PSU3F/4R built 1981
Body: Plaxton C53F

389	PNB 805W	390	PNB 806W	391	PNB 807W

400-426

Chassis: DAF MB200DKTL600 built 1982
Body: Plaxton C51F

400	TND 400X	406	TND 406X	412	TND 412X	418	TND 418X
401	TND 401X	407	TND 407X	413	TND 413X	419	TND 419X
402	TND 402X	408	TND 408X	414	TND 414X	420	TND 420X
403	TND 403X	409	TND 409X	415	TND 415X	421	TND 421X
404	TND 404X	410	TND 410X	416	TND 416X	426	TND 426X
405	TND 405X	411	TND 411X	417	TND 417X		

431

Chassis: Volvo B10M-56 built 1982
Body: Plaxton C51F

431   TND 431X

Smiths Happiway Spencers Ltd

Smith's Tours of Wigan has been operating since at least 1921, in which year they owned a Pagefield charabanc. It is probable that Smith's began coaching work before the First World War. The other two companies whose names are reflected in the present title are also long established. Stanley Spencer was operating by 1919, and Happiway Tours of Manchester appears to have started in the late 1920s.

In the early 1950s Smith's Tours became part of the Gleave group, together with Florence Motors of Morecambe. Smith's was later sold to Mr Freddie Webster of Wigan, who amalgamated it with his own Webster's Coaches and sold the combined company to Blundells of Southport.

Blundell's Coaches (Southport) Ltd traced its ancestry to a taxi firm founded in the late 1940s by Hilda and Wilfred Blundell. During the 1950s they diversified into general haulage and coaching as well as their taxis; by the end of the decade they had decided to concentrate on coaching to the exclusion of the other activities. They expanded by buying Smith's Tours and Webster's in 1964. It is of interest that the 'bunch of flags' trademark, carried on the rear luggage lockers of all Smith's coaches during the 1950s and early 1960s, was retained by the Gleave group and is now used by Florence Motors. The group controlled by Blundell's had therefore to develop a new trademark, depicting a line of flags, which is still carried on the rear of all Group coaches.

In 1972 Smith's Tours bought out Happiway-Spencer Ltd of Manchester, which was itself a product of the amalgamation of Happiway Tours and Stanley Spencer's in the 1960s. Happiway-Spencer traded in the Manchester area, for many years being at 11/27 Lower Mosley Street near the erstwhile Bus Station. After the takeover, Happiway-Spencer moved to premises in Levenshulme which had been vacated by Hartley's Tours, which had also been taken over by Smith's. Other companies which became part of the Blundell Group were Hargreaves of Bolton and Smith's Atalanta of Blackpool.

The increasing size of the Blundell Group made it appear ripe for possible takeover itself. Greater Manchester PTE obtained an option to purchase a controlling interest in the Blundell Group, but never exercised their option, and in 1979 the option was sold back to the Blundell family and the families of the other directors. In April 1982, however, the entire group was purchased by Associated Leisure PLC, who own 9 hotels in leading seaside resorts in England and Scotland. These hotels will be easy to co-ordinate with the main activity of Blundell Group coaches, which is the operation of extended tours throughout Britain and the Continent. Under Associated Leisure management, one other coach company has been added to the Group - Kildare's of Adwick-le-Street, near Doncaster. By the time this appears in print it is expected that Kildare's own fleet, mainly of Leyland 'Leopards', will have been replaced by standard Group coaches operating from the Adwick depot.

Although coach tours are the main activity, several of the subsidiary companies, particularly Webster's, have works contracts which take up part of the fleet on weekdays. In the case of Webster's, these activities are dovetailed with the Group's only express coach operations, which run on summer Saturdays from

Wigan and neighbouring towns to Bridlington/Filey/Scarborough, Skegness, the Norfolk Coast resorts, Minehead, Torquay, Pwllheli and the North Wales resorts between Prestatyn and Llandudno.

While little is known about vehicles of the constituent companies in the early days, after the advent of the underfloor-engined coach the characteristic coach for Smith's Tours was the AEC Reliance with Plaxton bodywork; many of these were rebodied to prolong their lives. Happiway-Spencers ran a mixture of Leyland and various lightweight makes. Under Blundell control the emphasis switched to Fords, but AECs were still bought in quantity as well. About 1975 the group switched to Duple rather than Plaxton bodywork, and Duple remains standard today. Recent deliveries have included Volvo coaches, more of which are on order.

The various subsidiary companies still operate their own contracts and private hire, but Group practice is now to license all vehicles to the main company, Smiths-Happiway-Spencers Ltd, and allocate coaches to the various subsidiary depots as required. The subsidiaries are therefore operating, but not owning, companies. The head office is at 70 Market Street, Wigan. The main garage is at Gower Street, Wigan (Smith's and Webster's), with other garages at Adwickle-Street (Kildare's), Blackpool (Smith's Atalanta), Bolton (Hargreaves), Manchester (Happiway-Spencers) and Southport (Blundell's). There is also a large coach interchange at Cranage, on the A50 between Knutsford and Holmes Chapel. The livery has been changed in detail several times, and now consists of lower panels in topaz, upper panels in ivory, and orange lining-out at waist level. The fleetname 'SMITH'S HAPPIWAY SPENCERS' is currently giving way to 'SMITH'S HAPPIWAYS'.

35-37

Chassis: AEC 'Reliance' 6U3ZR built 1977
Body: Duple C53F

| 35 | ODJ 53R | 36 | REK 928R | 37 | REK 929R |

40

Chassis: AEC 'Reliance' 6U2R built 1977
Body: Duple C57F

| 40 | REK 927R |

45-46

Chassis: AEC 'Reliance' 6U3ZR built 1977
Body: Duple C53F

| 45 | REK 925R | 46 | REK 926R |

89-98

Chassis: AEC 'Reliance' 6U3ZR built 1978
Body: Duple C57F

89	WED 983S	92	WED 986S	95	WED 989S	97	WED 991S
90	WED 984S	93	WED 987S	96	WED 990S	98	WED 992S
91	WED 985S	94	WED 988S				

99-101

Chassis: Volvo B58-61 built 1979
Body: Duple C53F

| 99 | BTB 682T | 100 | BTB 683T | 101 | BTB 684T |

102-108

Chassis: AEC 'Reliance' 6U3ZR built 1979
Body: Duple C57F

| 102 | BTB 685T | 104 | BTB 687T | 106 | BTB 689T | 108 | BTB 691T |
| 103 | BTB 686T | 105 | BTB 688T | 107 | BTB 690T | | |

109-129

Chassis: Ford R1114 built 1979/1980
Body: Duple C53F

109	BTB 692T	115	BTB 698T	120	BTB 703T	125	HJP 474V
110	BTB 693T	116	BTB 699T	121	BTB 704T	126	HJP 475V
111	BTB 694T	117	BTB 700T	122	HJP 471V	127	HJP 476V
113	BTB 696T	118	BTB 701T	123	HJP 472V	128	HJP 477V
114	BTB 697T	119	BTB 702T	124	HJP 473V	129	HJP 478V

130-145

Chassis: Volvo B58-61 built 1979/1980
Body: Duple C53F

130	BTB 713T	134	HJP 480V	138	HJP 484V	142	HJP 488V
131	BTB 714T	135	HJP 481V	139	HJP 485V	143	HJP 489V
132	BTB 715T	136	HJP 482V	140	HJP 486V	144	HJP 490V
133	HJP 479V	137	HJP 483V	141	HJP 487V	145	HJP 498V

146-152

Chassis: Ford R1114 built 1980
Body: Duple C53F

146	HJP 492V	148	HJP 494V	150	HJP 496V	152	HJP 491V
147	HJP 493V	149	HJP 495V	151	HJP 497V		

153

Chassis: AEC 'Reliance' 2MU3RV built 1957, rebuilt and lengthened 1980
Body: Duple C45F built 1980
The chassis is believed to have belonged originally to JCN 449, new to Northern General Transport and acquired by Smith's from the Newcastle Scout Group (non-PSV) in 1980

    153   CDK 796V

154

Chassis: AEC 'Reliance' 6U3ZR built 1969
Body: Duple C53F built 1981

    154   LWM 475G

155

Chassis: Volvo B10M-61 built 1980
Body: Duple C53F
Registered by Volvo as a demonstrator for use at the 1980 Motor Show, but owned by Smith's from new

    155   JSJ 426W

156-165

Chassis: Volvo B58-61 built 1981
Body: Duple C53F

156	ODJ 575W	159	ODJ 578W	162	ODJ 581W	164	ODJ 583W
157	ODJ 576W	160	ODJ 579W	163	ODJ 582W	165	ODJ 584W
158	ODJ 577W	161	ODJ 580W				

166-196

Chassis: Ford R1114 built 1981/1982
Body: Duple C53F

166	ODJ 585W	174	ODJ 593W	182	ODJ 601W	190	TND 104X
167	ODJ 586W	175	ODJ 594W	183	ODJ 602W	191	TND 105X
168	ODJ 587W	176	ODJ 595W	184	ODJ 603W	192	TND 106X
169	ODJ 588W	177	ODJ 596W	185	ODJ 604W	193	TND 107X
170	ODJ 589W	178	ODJ 597W	186	ODJ 605W	194	TND 108X
171	ODJ 590W	179	ODJ 598W	187	TND 101X	195	TND 109X
172	ODJ 591W	180	ODJ 599W	188	TND 102X	196	TND 110X
173	ODJ 592W	181	ODJ 600W	189	TND 103X		

197-226

Chassis: Volvo B58-61 built 1982
Body: Duple C53F

197	TND 111X	205	TND 119X	213	TND 127X	220	TND 134X
198	TND 112X	206	TND 120X	214	TND 128X	221	TND 135X
199	TND 113X	207	TND 121X	215	TND 129X	222	TND 136X
200	TND 114X	208	TND 122X	216	TND 130X	223	TND 137X
201	TND 115X	209	TND 123X	217	TND 131X	224	TND 138X
202	TND 116X	210	TND 124X	218	TND 132X	225	TND 139X
203	TND 117X	211	TND 125X	219	TND 133X	226	TND 140X
204	TND 118X	212	TND 126X				

227-251

Chassis: Volvo B10M-61 on order 1983
Body: Duple C53F

227	234	240	246
228	235	241	247
229	236	242	248
230	237	243	249
231	238	244	250
232	239	245	251
233			

Chassis: Ford R1114 on order 1983
Body: Duple C53F
10 coaches (fleet numbers not yet available)

Chassis: Volvo B10M-61 on order 1983
Body: Van Hool C49F
5 coaches (fleet numbers not yet available)

Chassis: Ford 'Transit' built 1979/1980
Body: Tricentrol 12-seat
Fleet numbers are not allocated

BEK 238T   BEK 247T   BEK 272T   FJP 845V   JTB 137V

Yelloway Motor Services Ltd

The Yelloway name, which is now such a familiar sight on the distinctive cream and orange coaches, first appeared about 1930. Mr Herbert Allen, the firm's founder and the father of the present Managing Director, reconstructed a coach firm, Holt's of Bacup, which had fallen into financial difficulties as a result of the Depression. Thus Yelloway Motor Services Ltd was born.

Although Yelloway's main interest is in the operation of express coach services, the company operated a limited-stop stage carriage service between Rochdale and Manchester until 1944. In the summer of that year, however, the service was transferred to joint operation by Manchester, Oldham and Rochdale Corporations, who continued to operate it until transfer to SELNEC in 1969. It still runs today in the form of Greater Manchester services 23/24. Yelloway handed over several vehicles, including some double-deckers, to the three corporations in 1944 to cover the operation of this service.

A postwar feature was the development of a through service from North-West England to East Anglia, jointly with Premier Travel Ltd of Cambridge. This route now runs from Blackpool and the East Lancashire area, through Rochdale, Manchester, Derby, Leicester, Northampton, Bedford, Cambridge and Colchester to Clacton-on-Sea. In 1974 another route to East Anglia was started, originating in Liverpool and run jointly with both Premier Travel and National Travel. Other express routes now operated by Yelloway connect Greater Manchester and Central Lancashire to the South and South-West via Cheltenham, North and South Wales, and the Fylde Coast. A service exchange with National Travel in 1976 gave Yelloway sole operation of some of these services in exchange for Yelloway workings from Lancashire, Greater Manchester and Derbyshire to London.

In 1977 Yelloway was involved with Wallace Arnold and National Travel in extending the 'South-West Clipper' services from Yorkshire through to Bournemouth and later to Portsmouth. In 1978 the company helped National Travel (East) and Premier Travel to pioneer a new service between Sheffield and Clacton/Harwich.

In the early post-war years AECs replaced Leylands as the mainstay of the fleet, although from time to time Bedfords have been owned as well. With the demise of the AEC 'Reliance', which has been Yelloway's standard coach since it was first produced, the company took delivery in 1980 of four Leyland 'Leopards', its first-ever vehicles of this type; four more 'Leopards' arrived in 1981 and two 'Tigers' in 1982. The AEC 'Reliance' accounts for the whole of the rest of the fleet. The company has successively favoured Burlingham, Duple, Harrington and Plaxton bodywork, and Plaxton's account for all but two coaches in stock at present. Many vehicles are fitted with adjustable reclining seats, a special Yelloway feature offering a superior standard of comfort on long journeys. The garage, head office and principal coach station are all located at Weir Street, Rochdale, opposite Rochdale bus station.

		Chassis:	AEC 'Reliance' 6U3ZR (12-metre) built 1971/1972		
		Body:	Plaxton C53F (TDK 689J is C45F with reclining seats)		
TDK 684J	TDK 686J	TDK 689J	WDK 646K	WDK 647K	WDK 648K
TDK 685J	TDK 687J	WDK 645K			

		Chassis:	AEC 'Reliance' 6U3ZR (11-metre) built 1972/1973
		Body:	Plaxton C45F with reclining seats (CDK 172L is C49F with fixed seats)
	WDK 649K	WDK 650K	CDK 171L CDK 172L

	Chassis:	AEC 'Reliance' 6U3ZR (12-metre) built 1973-1975
	Body:	(CDK 173-175L, RDK 428M, HVU 243N) Plaxton C53F with fixed seats
		(Remainder) Plaxton C49F with reclining seats